COMPLETE INSTRUMENTAL CHAMBER WORKS

RECENT RESEARCHES IN THE MUSIC OF THE NINETEENTH AND EARLY TWENTIETH CENTURIES

Rufus Hallmark, general editor

A-R Editions, Inc., publishes seven series of musicological editions that present music brought to light in the course of current research:

Recent Researches in the Music of the Middle Ages and Early Renaissance
Charles M. Atkinson, general editor

Recent Researches in the Music of the Renaissance
James Haar, general editor

Recent Researches in the Music of the Baroque Era
Christoph Wolff, general editor

Recent Researches in the Music of the Classical Era
Eugene K. Wolf, general editor

Recent Researches in the Music of the Nineteenth and Early Twentieth Centuries
Rufus Hallmark, general editor

Recent Researches in American Music
John M. Graziano, general editor

Recent Researches in the Oral Traditions of Music
Philip V. Bohlman, general editor

Each *Recent Researches* edition is devoted to works by a single composer or to a single genre of composition. The contents are chosen for their potential interest to scholars and performers, then prepared for publication according to the standards that govern the making of all reliable historical editions.

Subscribers to any of these series, as well as patrons of subscribing institutions, are invited to apply for information about the "Copyright-Sharing Policy" of A-R Editions, Inc., under which policy any part of an edition may be reproduced free of charge for study or performance.

For information contact

A-R EDITIONS, INC.
801 Deming Way
Madison, Wisconsin 53717

(800) 736-0070 (U.S. book orders)
(608) 836-9000 (phone)
(608) 831-8200 (fax)
areditions@aol.com (e-mail)

RECENT RESEARCHES IN THE MUSIC OF THE NINETEENTH
AND EARLY TWENTIETH CENTURIES • VOLUME 24

Walter Rabl

COMPLETE INSTRUMENTAL CHAMBER WORKS

Edited by John F. and Virginia F. Strauss

A-R Editions, Inc.
Madison

Performance parts are available from the publisher.

© 1996 by A-R Editions, Inc.
All rights reserved
Printed in the United States of America

ISBN 0-89579-332-6
ISSN 0193-5364

∞The paper used in this publication meets the minimum requirements
of the American National Standard for Information Sciences—Permanence
of Paper for Printed Library Materials, ANSI Z39.48-1984.

Contents

PREFACE	vii
The Composer and His Music	vii
The Music of the Edition	x
Sources and Editorial Methods	xi
Critical Notes	xii
Acknowledgments	xii
Notes	xiii
PLATES	xv

Quartet, Op. 1
for piano, violin, clarinet (or viola), and violoncello

I. Allegro moderato	1
II. Adagio molto	18
III. Andantino un poco mosso	30
IV. Allegro con brio	35

Fantasiestücke, Op. 2
for piano, violin, and violoncello

1. Adagio molto	60
2. Allegro vivace	62
3. Allegro con spirito	69
4. Adagio con espressione	71
5. Allegro con impeto	74
6. Allegretto grazioso	81
7. Largo	86
8. Allegro vivace con brio	91

Sonata, Op. 6
for piano and violin

[I] Allegro moderato, ma energico	109
[II] Adagio con espressione	135
[III] Allegretto grazioso	141
[IV] Allegro vivace	147

Appendix 1: Viola Part for the Quartet, Op. 1	169
Appendix 2: Catalog of Walter Rabl's Published Works	179

Preface

Like his contemporaries Franz Schmidt, Franz Schreker, and Alexander von Zemlinsky (all beneficiaries of the fin de siècle Vienna revival), Walter Rabl (1873–1940) wrote large-scale, harmonically sumptuous works that recall the vanishing golden age of Viennese romanticism. He began as a disciple of Johannes Brahms and moved gradually, especially in his vocal writing, into the camp of Richard Wagner. Although Rabl lived well into the twentieth century, the opera *Liane* (1903) was his last published work.

The music of this edition includes the prize-winning Quartet for piano, violin, clarinet (or viola), and violoncello, op. 1 (the only piece of nineteenth-century chamber music scored for this combination), two volumes of *Fantasiestücke* for piano, violin, and violoncello, op. 2, and the Sonata for piano and violin, op. 6. All three works were originally published in Berlin by the Simrock publishing house, which also supported and promoted the careers of Johannes Brahms, Antonín Dvořák, and Johann Strauss.

Walter Rabl's chamber works are not only historically interesting because of the composer's relationship to Johannes Brahms; they also deserve the attention of contemporary historians and theorists for intrinsic musical reasons. The melodies, harmonies, textures, linear writing, handling of large-scale forms, and Romantic expression mirror the Vienna of the 1890s, where Rabl's musical tastes were formed. At the time they were written, Rabl's chamber works were recognized for their excellence not only by Brahms and the Simrock firm, but also by newspaper critics and contemporary audiences. Rudolf Felber concludes a short entry about Walter Rabl in the 1929 edition of *Cobbett's Cyclopedic Survey of Chamber Music* with these words: "Rabl's chamber works are influenced by both Schumann and Brahms, but they are fresh and enjoyable compositions of considerable artistic worth, clear and simple in form, thoroughly natural and unforced in expression."[1]

The Composer and His Music

Walter Rabl was born in Vienna on 30 November 1873, the son of *Regierungsrat Dr. med.* Johannes Rabl and Rosine Bernard. The family lived in Herrengasse 12 at the back of the Neue Hofburg. Little is known about Rabl's childhood, except that he graduated from the Kaiserlich und Königlich Staatsgymnasium of Salzburg with distinction in 1892, and that he expressed an intention to study law. While in Salzburg, he also studied theory and composition with J. F. Hummel, director of the Mozarteum, and became an accomplished pianist. According to a monograph written by A. Eccarius-Sieber in 1907, Rabl was familiar with the works of the classical masters from an astonishingly early age and was decisively influenced by them.[2]

Rabl's theoretical studies continued along classical lines with Carl Navratil in Vienna. Although clearly an acolyte of Brahms at this stage of his life, Rabl may have first encountered the music of Gustav Mahler and Richard Strauss, composers he was later to ardently champion, in the middle 1890s. Rabl also enrolled in a Ph.D. program at the German University of Prague and became a special student of the eminent and progressive musicologist Guido Adler. Adler lost no time in enlisting Walter Rabl and another young composer, Anton von Webern, as researchers for his monumental eighty-eight volume series Denkmäler der Tonkunst in Österreich.[3]

In 1896, while still a doctoral candidate without a clear professional calling, Rabl decided to enter a prestigious competition for young composers. Since 1886, Brahms had been honorary president of the Wiener Tonkünstlerverein, a society that periodically offered composition prizes to further the course of musical culture.[4] The competition that Rabl entered was the fourth offered by the Tonkünstlerverein and the last in which Brahms himself participated. The announcement called for new chamber works containing at least one wind part.

Brahms played an active role in virtually all aspects—musical, scholarly, and financial—of the Tonkünstlerverein and served as the de facto head of its composition juries. An avid book and manuscript collector as well as a painstaking editor of numerous music editions,[5] Brahms was also interested in the future of music, tirelessly promoting, criticizing, and teaching promising young composers.[6] Eduard Hanslick, Brahms's long-time friend and music critic of the *Neue freie Presse*, wrote in 1899:

> As honorary president of the *Wiener Tonkünstlerverein*, whose evening receptions he attended regularly and with pleasure, he was a zealous promoter of competitions, especially chamber music competitions, to bring young talents to the fore. When it came to the examination of the anonymous manuscripts that had been submitted, he showed astonishing acuity in guessing from the overall impression and technical details, who the author was, or at least his school or teacher. Last year Brahms was very interested in an anonymous quartet whose author he was quite unable to identify. Impatiently he waited for the opening of the sealed notice. On it was written the heretofore entirely unknown name: Walter Rabl.[7]

On 3 December 1896, Brahms wrote to his friend and publisher Fritz Simrock:

> If there is any money for me in Berlin, it can be put in the *Reichskeller*, as there is still enough of the English inheritance on hand, even though I am endowing the

prize-winning compositions royally. All of them should be performed by December 11 and subsequently voted on. In any case, the best piece is a piano quartet with clarinet. It is supposed to be by Rabl, a student of Navratil. I know little of the young man and his work, as I did not much care for him [on first meeting]. Of course, now, I will keep an eye on him and his piece.[8]

The competition took place as planned with Brahms, Eusebius Mandyczewski,[9] and Richard von Perger sitting as judges. Of the eighteen compositions submitted, twelve were performed at the expense of the Tonkünstlerverein. Brahms himself contributed money to the three prizes, which went to Walter Rabl (first prize for the Quartet, op. 1), Joseph Miroslav Weber (second prize), and Alexander von Zemlinsky (third prize for the Trio, op. 3).[10]

Brahms clearly valued the compositions by Rabl and Weber more highly than that of Zemlinsky. Yet most historical accounts of Brahms's life mention the latter and ignore the former. For example, in a recent biography of Brahms, Malcolm MacDonald writes:

> Brahms's attention was attracted by a Trio in D minor for clarinet, cello and piano composed, in obvious but highly gifted emulation of his own Clarinet Trio, by the twenty-four-year-old Alexander von Zemlinsky, who had studied at the *Gesellschaft der Musikfreunde* and was now member of the *Tonkünstlerverein* (of which Brahms was honorary president). Brahms not only gave Zemlinsky advice but, in one of his last acts of generosity to a young musician, induced Simrock to publish the Trio and its equally impressive successor, the First String Quartet.[11]

Rabl, the first prize winner, is never mentioned by MacDonald, or indeed by other recent biographers of Brahms.

On 17 December 1896, Brahms wrote again to Simrock:

> I will report ever more pleasant things about our prize-winning composer Walter Rabl. I have at home a substantial pile of his works. He himself will arrive soon for the [prize awarding] ceremony; he is in the process of obtaining his doctorate in Prague. The voting will be held on the 22d [of December]; I think he will get the first prize—but this is really unimportant. Everything will be taken care of by yours, J. B.[12]

Brahms's next reference to Rabl appears in a letter dated 23 December: "By the way, Mr. Rabl did win the first prize. So far as you are concerned, everything will be taken care of, about which he is very happy."[13] Brahms's final reference to Rabl was made on 31 December:

> You have an extraordinary desire for new things. The quartet by Rabl and the trio by Zemlinsky are yours. In both instances I can recommend the person and the talent. If Rabl is hesitant about sending you the quartet, it is my fault, as he was led to think that he should wait until he can enclose or immediately follow it up with works of equal worth.[14]

Rabl responded shortly thereafter, and in 1897, Simrock published not only the quartet but also two books of *Fantasiestücke*, op. 2, *Vier Lieder*, op. 3, and *Vier Lieder*, op. 4. In 1899, a second series of works was published: *Vier Lieder*, op. 5, *Sonate für Pianoforte und Violine*, op. 6, *Drei Lieder*, op. 7, and *Symphonie für grosses Orchester*, op. 8.

In his monograph, Eccarius-Sieber quotes Hans von Bülow's well-known remark—"the more prizes a work wins, the more it fails"—and then admits that in Rabl's case this observation is not true. At its premier in December 1897, the quartet was well received by the public and music cognoscenti alike and impressed people as the work of a mature artist.[15]

Encouraged by his early successes, Rabl set out to make his career in music. At the age of twenty-five, he completed his doctorate and began work as a volunteer at the opera in Prague. A few months later, he was hired as opera coach and chorus master (*Korrepetitor*) at the Royal Opera of Dresden, where he remained until 1902. His next series of compositions, all lieder, beginning with the *Frau Sehnsucht*, op. 9, and continuing through the *Zwei Lieder*, op. 15, were published by D. Rahter of Leipzig.[16]

In September 1903, Rabl made his debut as kapellmeister at the state theater of Düsseldorf, where he worked with great diligence until 1906 under the direction of Ludwig Zimmermann. Between 1906 and the outbreak of World War I, Rabl conducted operas in Essen, Dortmund, Breslau, and in other opera houses throughout Germany. He also courted and married Hermine von Kriesten, a Wagnerian soprano and the daughter of a Hungarian aristocrat.

Hermine Rabl von Kriesten, as she called herself after her marriage in 1905, was becoming a singer of prominence at that time. She sang under the direction of Rabl in Düsseldorf, Essen, and Dortmund, but also at the Hofoper (now the Staatsoper) in Vienna under the direction of Bruno Walter, Felix Weingartner, Richard Strauss, and other conductors. Hofoper programs from the 1910 and 1911 seasons show that she always sang major roles: Brünnhilde in *Die Walküre, Siegfried,* and *Götterdämmerung;* Elektra in *Elektra;* the Queen in *Die Königin von Saba* (Goldmark); and Leonore in *Fidelio.* At first she was listed as a guest artist from the Stadttheater in Breslau; later she appeared as part of the regular Hofoper company. So frequently did she sing the role of Elektra during the 1910 and 1911 seasons that it must have seemed to the Viennese public that the role was reserved exclusively for her. Then in 1911 she had a serious disagreement with the Hofoper director, Felix Weingartner, who peremptorily replaced her with Lucille Marcel. Marcel, "mit grossen Kinderaugen [und] Grübchen in den Wangen,"[17] became not only the new Elektra but also Weingartner's third wife.

Shortly after the turn of the century, Rabl ceased composing lieder and turned to writing opera. The result, *Liane,* marked a turning point in the composer's life. Eccarius-Sieber, reflecting the opinions of the contemporary press, wrote:

In larger circles of the musical world, conductor and composer Dr. Walter Rabl has made himself known through performances of his romantic fairy tale opera *Liane*. Since this opera in its entire design and setting follows the Wagnerian artistic style while Walter Rabl—award-winning composer of a beautiful clarinet quartet—previously had been considered to belong to the Brahms faction, its appearance had to draw considerable attention.[18]

Eccarius-Sieber followed his assertion with a brief biography, a discussion of Rabl's Brahms-influenced compositions, and a description of *Liane*, which he characterized as being Wagnerian in musical philosophy, size, and technical difficulty. "To date," he concluded, "*Liane* remains Rabl's most important work."[19]

Published in 1903, *Liane* received its premiere in Strasbourg, where it was acclaimed by music critics as an important new work by a master composer. The *Elsässer Volksbote* called *Liane* an "unmitigated joy and complete success," mentioning its Wagnerian modernity: "The composer has complete command of the modern orchestra; particular attention, it appeared to me, had been given to the string section."[20] The *Straßburger Post* reported that "We doubtlessly have in Walter Rabl a composer who has entered the sphere of modern art that is based on traditional classical culture and who is in complete command of its techniques and [artistic] devices."[21] The *Straßburger Zeitung* went still further: "Despite leaning occasionally on the unmistakable model of Richard Wagner, we are confident that Walter Rabl has entered into the ranks of the few musicians on whom the hope of the future rests."[22] The *Straßburger Neuste Nachrichten* continued in the same vein: "We are indeed confronted here with a rare and beautiful work. The musical language is so noble, so deeply felt that it is equal to nothing less than the wonderful expression of Richard Wagner.... Nowhere is there even the slightest hint of a trivial phrase!"[23] Two years later, in Düsseldorf, the press was still enthusiastic: "The success of the work was—judging by the reaction of the audience—unequivocally great. We believe that *Liane* will remain constant in the repertoire of our opera, standing unique as a decorative stage piece. After the applause and infinite shower of flowers..., the director/composer Dr. Walter Rabl covered with laurels appeared before the stage apron."[24]

Eccarius-Sieber wrote most of his 1907 monograph around a description and analysis of *Liane*. It was natural, he argued, that Rabl, constantly occupied with stage work, should turn his compositional efforts to opera. His immersion in musical drama, and especially in the works of Wagner, caused an artistic reversal in his thinking: "Thus we encounter the one-time Brahms disciple and *Quartett* composer now among the poets of the opera."[25]

Rabl, however, may have felt otherwise. The composer's son, Dr. Kurt Rabl (born 1909), in a letter to the editors of this edition, suggests the following:

> As a composer, he had stopped writing long before the outbreak of World War I. His last work, an opera (*Liane*, based on the attractive and romantic book of a subtle Dresden lyricist Wilhelm Eberhard Ernst) was, as he once told me, rightfully characterized by the critics after its world premiere as unmistakably Wagnerian. He came to the (exaggeratedly?) self-critical conclusion that as a composer he lacked creativity and that it was proper, therefore, to forgo further efforts in this area. Perhaps he felt that he had been untrue to the Brahms tradition, that he had joined the all-too-numerous Wagnerian epigones.[26]

If Rabl ceased composing and performing his own works, he seemingly redoubled his efforts on behalf of other late-romantic composers. Wagner, Mahler, Bruckner, Schreker, Korngold, and his friend Richard Strauss were prominently represented on his orchestral programs. He also accompanied lieder recitals with great frequency. "He was a divinely gifted pianist," writes Dr. Kurt Rabl, "highly esteemed and much sought after by many famous lieder interpreters of his day (Maria Ivogün, Lauritz Melchior, Heinrich Knothe, Heinrich Schlusnus, and many others). I myself owe the most vivid memories of my youth to lieder concerts at which he accompanied compositions by Brahms, Schubert (*Winterreise!*), or Wolf on the piano."[27]

Beginning in 1907 and continuing until the outbreak of World War I, Rabl also directed German operas each summer and occasionally during the normal opera season at the Teatro Real in Madrid.[28] Rabl was effusively praised in the Spanish press for introducing Wagner to Spain. Due in large part to his many performances of *Der Ring des Niebelungen*, a Wagnerian association was established in Madrid. Presided over by the duke of Alba, the association numbered twelve hundred people by December 1911, when Rabl was invited back for a gala performance at the Teatro Real. He also conducted *Salome, Der Rosenkavalier,* and at least some Italian and French opera, including *Aida* and *Hamlet*. (Frau Rabl von Kriesten was criticized in the press for not being proficient in Italian.) Rabl last appeared in Madrid on 18 December 1923, conducting *Tristan und Isolde*, and on 5 January 1924, conducting *Der Rosenkavalier*.

Rabl's last important conducting post was in Magdeburg, where he was appointed first city kapellmeister in 1915. He conducted both opera and symphony subscription concerts in a city that was devastated first by war and then by economic disaster. Rabl conducted the standard literature from Beethoven to Mahler and Strauss and introduced *Parsifal* to the city. According to the 1987 pamphlet, *Stadtisches Orchester Magdeburg, Parsifal* was performed thirty-two times between its Magdeburg premiere on 18 April 1920 and 8 June 1921. "As city opera and concert director, his special contribution was to establish Bruckner and the new Romantics (Schreker, Korngold) in the repertoire."[29]

In 1924, Rabl was succeeded by Walter Beck (1890–1966), "apparently because he [Rabl] was too conservative, both musically and politically."[30] In 1926, after refusing for several years to join the political party that held a majority in the city parliament, Rabl lost not only his Magdeburg position but also other conducting opportunities in the Ruhr. Although the *Österreichisches Biographisches Lexikon* mentions that there were tours to the United States and Canada after 1929, these too were canceled. "After he was relieved from his duties by the community in 1926, he nonetheless remained there [Magdeburg] as a popular and much sought-after piano and theory teacher until his death in 1940."

The Music of the Edition

Rabl's three early chamber works are notable examples of music embodying the principles of the conservative romantic style as practiced by Schumann and Brahms. In his recent biography of Brahms, MacDonald describes the mission of the conservative romantic composer as follows:

> His special destiny was to reconcile . . . Romanticism's conflicting musical demands for intense expression of feeling *and* for closeness to the spirit of the oldest, "purest" music; and to synthesize these with a revived mastery of the large-scale dynamics of Classical structure.[31]

The Quartet, op. 1, published in 1897 and dedicated to Brahms, is a monument to conservative romanticism in its synthesis of intense expression and classical structure.

The scoring, prompted by the rules of the Brahms contest (piano, violin, clarinet, and cello), is unique in nineteenth-century chamber music literature. Rabl's colorful handling of the instrumentation is in part responsible for the expressivity of the work. With just four instruments, he is able to create dramatic textural contrasts: on the one hand, there are intimate solo moments, such as the opening three phrases of the first movement, and on the other, there are glorious symphonic tuttis, as in the "Lento grandioso" (m. 87) at the climax of the second movement.

Rabl also uses creative voicing to enlarge his textural vocabulary. For example, the first full-ensemble statement of the main theme of the first movement (mm. 33–48), where he places the violin, clarinet, and cello in their lowest to middle ranges to support the piano melody in its highest range, creates a full texture, but not one that might overshadow the dramatically richer textures to come. In addition, elaborate doublings, piano arpeggiation, and string double stops suggest harmonic complexity. Seven-, eight-, and nine-note chords in the piano and a three-octave spread between the other parts are not uncommon in dense passages, such as in measures 51–54 in the fourth movement.

On a more detailed level, Rabl's instrumentation skills enhance the expressive qualities of the Quartet. The instruments are treated idiomatically, exploring their full pitch and dynamic ranges. The dark, sustained sound of the clarinet, for example, is used to advantage in the second theme of the first movement (m. 65) and for the melody (over the violin and cello) of the first variation in the second movement (m. 9). Rabl also takes advantage of idiomatic string instrument colors, such as the use of natural harmonics for the highest, most delicate notes in the violin melody of the third movement (m. 17 and m. 34). He uses double stops for thickening textures and for special effects, such as the hollow perfect fifth cello drone that underlies the melancholic second theme of the first movement (m. 65).

Rabl's idiomatic writing for the piano in particular reflects the composer's familiarity with romantic virtuoso techniques, such as the five-voice simple chordal accompaniment for the main theme of the third movement, the contrary motion octave arpeggiation, which rhythmically controls the first variation of the second movement (m. 9), and the flamboyant, filled-in octave passages, which pervade the most grandiose moments of the work, such as the codas to the first (m. 293) and last (m. 191) movements.

In form and tonal organization, the Quartet meets the second requirement of the conservative romantic style described by MacDonald: "the mastery of the large-scale dynamics of Classical structure." It is a substantial four-movement work following the inherited classical pattern with the first movement (Allegro moderato, E-flat major) in sonata form, the second (Adagio molto, C minor) in theme and variations form, the third (Andantino un poco mosso, G major) in ABA' form, and the fourth (Allegro con brio, E-flat major) in sonata form. Classical proportions also dictate the shape of the various sections within each movement, which are clearly delineated by thematic material and key.

Rabl's reverence for music of the past is reflected in his skillful linear writing, especially in its motivic organization. A cursory motivic analysis of the opening sixty-three measures (first theme and bridge) of the first movement serves to illustrate Rabl's Beethoven-like substructure and flow of musical ideas: mm. 1–8, the first theme (clarinet); mm. 9–16, a tonal expansion of the theme (violin); mm. 17–24, the first half of the theme twice (cello); mm. 25–28, a two-measure contraction of the theme in diminution with imitation (ensemble); mm. 29–32, the first four notes of the theme reduced to even eighth notes with imitation (ensemble); mm. 33–48, a full statement of two phrases of the first theme (piano); mm. 49–52, the four-note motive from measure 29 in quarter notes in imitation (piano and clarinet); mm. 53–56, the four-note motive in eighth notes in a chain (piano and clarinet); mm. 57–60, the four-note motive inverted in augmentation and extended one note (cello and violin); mm. 61–63, the first two notes of the inverted motive in a chain (violin).

In addition to its traditional form and motivic organization, the Quartet exhibits a classical tonal organization with a strong sense of tonal center both within and between movements. Secondary key areas are generally closely related to the primary key, such as the E-flat major first theme and C minor second theme in the first movement, or the E-flat major first theme and B-flat major second theme of the last movement. While there is much free harmonic exploration and chromatic modulation in Rabl's developments, the inevitable return to the primary key is grandly set up with a traditional dominant to tonic progression, as, for example, the four-measure B-flat pedal (mm. 123–26) that leads to the E-flat return in measure 127 of the last movement.

An interesting feature of the Quartet is the alternative viola part, which can replace the clarinet. Since the viola line does not exist in the first edition score, and since the first edition viola part is riddled with errors (perhaps never proofread or played), it seems likely that it was an afterthought, perhaps recommended by the publisher to enhance sales. A note-by-note comparison of the original clarinet and alternative viola parts reveals many significant differences in the treatment of the two instruments and again points to Rabl's skill in instrumentation. The original viola part is published as an appendix to this edition.

Just as the Quartet emulates the large instrumental forms of Brahms, the *Fantasiestücke*, op. 2, recalls the song and piano cycles of Robert Schumann. In this work, one can appreciate Rabl from a different perspective, namely through his mastery of the large-scale tonal structure of a nineteenth-century cyclic form.

The *Fantasiestücke*, also published in 1897 but with no dedication, consists of eight pieces divided into two separately printed books (five pieces in the first and three in the second). The first book, with its contrasting moods and dramatic ending, might have originally been conceived as a complete work. However, the cyclical features that relate the second book to the first, the tonal structure, and a publisher's footnote[32] suggest that Rabl intended the eight-movement work to be performed as a whole.

The *Fantasiestücke* is scored for piano trio (violin, cello, and piano), an ensemble that was historically used (by Beethoven and Brahms, for instance) for traditional three- and four-movement large-scale works. Rabl's choice of this scoring for a set of character pieces is an unusual integration of a classical scoring and a romantic form. Like the great song and piano cycles of Schumann, the individual pieces that make up the *Fantasiestücke* are fairly short, use generally simple forms (i.e., through-composed or ABA form), and have distinctive, contrasting characters.

The large-scale structure of the work is modeled on the conservative romantic concept of the cycle as a whole, using Schumannesque techniques to achieve cohesiveness. Rabl sets the work in E major, with the first and eighth pieces in the tonic key and the others in a sequence of keys related by descending thirds. In the first piece, he uses Schumann's technique of undermining the tonal stability by deliberately avoiding the tonic chord in root position, except in the last four measures. The eighth piece functions as the major point of arrival in the large-scale structure of the *Fantasiestücke*, both tonally and thematically. It is the one long piece in the set, employing a fully developed sonata form with an elaborate coda, in which the opening thirteen measures of the first piece are integrated.

The Sonata, op. 6, for violin and piano is dedicated to Rabl's "revered teacher, Theodor Schwendt." Like the Quartet, it is a four movement work, symphonic in proportions and grandiose in spirit and thematic treatment. In the Sonata, one sees the same conservative romantic style that characterizes Rabl's writing in the Quartet and the *Fantasiestücke*: intense expression, technical competence, reverence for music of the past, and the inventive handling of traditional forms.

The key of the Sonata is D major, well chosen for the violin, because of the way in which it allows the composer to utilize the bright sound and natural harmonics of all the open strings. Rabl makes a great point of this in his selection of a perfect-fifth motive on D and A for the principal theme of the last movement.

As in the Quartet, the formal and tonal structures, both large- and small-scale, of the Sonata are traditional. The fourth movement, for example, is in sonata form, and well illustrates Rabl's inventiveness. He manipulates the musical material of the movement to give the impression of a more complex form. For instance, the first theme is presented as a three-voice fugue, which creates more the aura of a development than an exposition. The effect of perceived complexity is even more pronounced in the recapitulation.

The manner of expression and other stylistic details of the Sonata are so similar to those of his other early chamber works that they do not need illustration here, save for one aspect. There is a much greater level of virtuosity in Rabl's writing for the violin in this piece than in either the Quartet or the *Fantasiestücke*. The melody in octaves at the recapitulation of the first movement (mm. 133–40) is one example; another is the complex double-stop passage in the second movement (mm. 63–64), and yet another, the simultaneous arco and left-hand pizzicato in the third movement (mm. 77–80). In general, there is also more writing in the highest range of the fingerboard, such as the passage on the E string in the development of the first movement (mm. 85–89). Clearly, this piece was written for virtuoso players.

Sources and Editorial Methods

The three works edited in this volume were originally published by Simrock in Berlin in 1897 (the Quartet and the *Fantasiestücke*) and 1899 (the Sonata). Copies of the original editions used in the preparation of this edition are found in the Gesellschaft der Musikfreunde, Vienna (the Quartet), and the Staatsbibliothek zu Berlin, Preußischer Kulturbesitz (the *Fantasiestücke* and the Sonata).

Many trademarks of nineteenth-century German publications are in evidence in the original publications, such as periods after most words (abbreviated or not), interchangeable uppercase and lowercase letters (such as *Tempo* or *tempo*), and inconsistent placement, spelling, and abbreviation of form, tempo, dynamic, and expression marks. These idiosyncracies have all been regularized and modernized in the present edition. The original beaming has been retained. To facilitate the use of this edition, measure numbers have been added, and titles (except for *Fantasiestücke*) and part names have been given in English.

The first edition scores, especially those of the Quartet and the Sonata, lack the detailed performance directions found in the parts, and these differences have been taken from the parts and added to the present edition without editorial comment. A few serious errors in the sources (such as incorrect clefs, notes, and rhythms) have been changed in the edition and reported in the critical notes. The position of ties and slurs has been modernized without further comment. Accidentals and triplet labels have also been regularized and modernized tacitly. Shorthand notation in the original piano part (to denote repeated sixteenth-note chords) has been written out in the present edition. Editorial additions are placed in brackets or, in the case of slurs and ties, are dashed.

Critical Notes

The critical notes report readings in either the score or the parts that have been altered, including the elimination of extraneous or repetitive marks. Dynamic marks, expression marks, etc., that appear in the parts but not the score have been added to the edition without editorial indication. The abbreviations used in the critical notes are as follows: M(m). = measure(s); Vn. = violin; Cl. = clarinet; Vc. = violoncello; Pn. = piano. Pitch is indicated by the system in which c′ = middle C.

Quartet, Op. 1

I

M. 55, Vc., accent over tied notes in first beat. M. 85, Pn. has "sim." directive. M. 99, Pn., *8va* directive begins at note 1, with notes 1–3 written an octave down from present edition. M. 137, Vc., "tranquillo et espress." M. 157, Vn., notes 1–2 have diminuendo; *p* from m. 158 (see note for m. 158). M. 158, Vn., note 1 has *p*. M. 164, Pn., "sim." originally in m. 165. M. 240, Cl., whole rest in addition to c″ dotted half note.

II

M. 36, Cl., note 13 is a quarter note. M. 84, Vc., first beat is quarter note on g. M. 84, Vc., note 3, a♭ quarter note followed by eighth-note rest.

III

Mm. 3, 9, 11, Cl., notes 3–5 are slurred. M. 17, Cl., note 1 has *mf*. M. 35, Vc., slur over notes 5 and 6. M.58, Vn., Cl., Vc., no *ff* under note 2 (see note for m. 59). M. 59, Vn., Cl., Vc., note 1 has *ff*. M. 59, Pn., right hand, note 1, b dotted quarter note. M. 63, Vc., *ff* under note 2. M. 86, Vc., no *f* under note 1 (see note for m. 87). M. 87, Vc., note 1 has *f*. M. 88, Vc., no *f* under note 1 (see note for m. 89). M. 89, Vc., note 1 has *f*. M. 132, Cl., no *p* under note 1 (see note for m. 133). M. 133, Cl., note 1 has *p*. M. 138, Cl., note 1 has *mf*. Mm. 143–44, Cl., slur from note 1, m. 143 to note 1, m. 144. M. 188, Vc., quarter note on b♭, eighth-note rest, quarter-note rest, eighth-note rest. M. 190, Vc., whole-note rest.

Fantasiestücke, Op. 2

1

M. 9, Vn., note 2 through m. 10, notes 1–4, written down an octave with *8va* sign.

6

M. 58, Pn., left hand, note 1, flat on GG. M. 7, Vc., note 2 is c♮′.

7

M. 32, beat 2, higher note is g, not b.

8

M. 129, Pn., left hand, no ♮ before C.

Sonata, Op. 6

[I]

M. 134, Pn., right hand, notes 9–14, d–c–b–a–g–f. M. 161, Vn., note 1 has *p*. M. 170, Vn., note 1 has *mf*. M. 186, Vn., note 1 has *f*. M. 224, Vn., first beat has *ff*.

[III]

M. 139–40, Vn., "sul la" moved from m. 140, note 1 to m. 139, note 1. M. 62, Vn., notes 3 and 4 are g′. M. 334, Vn., slur extends to note 1 of m. 335. M. 354, Vn., slur extends to note 1 of m. 357. M. 360, Vn., slur extends to note 1 of m. 361. M. 367–68, Vn., slur extends from note 1 of m. 367 to note 8 of m. 368. M. 372, Vn., slur extends to note 1 of m. 373.

Acknowledgments

We would like to express our gratitude to John Strauss's father, the late historian Dr. Felix F. Strauss, for his help in obtaining and translating documents and for his untiring interest in our research; to Dr. Eva Wagner who located Walter Rabl's death certificate and led us to his son; to Dr. Kurt Rabl for providing us with two scores, various press releases, and helping us fill in biographical gaps; to Dr. J. Leon Helguera-Seis for translating portions of *Historia y Anecdotario del Teatro Real*; to *Chamber Music America* for allowing us to reprint several paragraph portions of John Strauss's earlier article, "Walter Rabl, the Brahms Prize and a Quartet op. 1" (summer 1990); to Dr. Ruth Kath for assisting with translation; to Dr. Mary Hull Mohr and Dr. Peter Liermann for assisting with proofreading; and above all to the Staatsbibliothek zu Berlin, Preussischer Kulturbesitz and the archive of the Gesellschaft der Musikfreunde, Vienna, who permitted us to publish this edition based on the scores in their collections.

Notes

1. Walter Willson Cobbett, *Cobbett's Cyclopedic Survey of Chamber Music* (London: Oxford University Press, 1929), 2:264.

2. A. Eccarius-Sieber, *Monographien Moderner Musiker: 20 Biographien zeitgenössischer Tonsetzer mit Portraits*, vol. 2 (Leipzig: C. F. Kahnt Nachfolger, 1907), is the richest source of information for Rabl's early years. Brief biographical entries are also found in the *Deutsches Musiker-Lexikon* (Dresden: W. Limpert, 1929), the *Kurzgefaßtes Tonkünstler-Lexikon* (Regensburg: G. Bosse, 1936), the *Österreichisches Biographisches Lexikon 1815–1950* (Vienna: Verlag der Österreichischen Akademie der Wissenschaften, 1983), and the *Universalhandbuch der Musikliteratur aller Völker*, vol. 24-1 (Vienna: Verlag des Universalhandbuch der Musikliteratur, n.d.). *Baker's Biographical Dictionary of Musicians*, 6th ed., has a brief entry on Walter Rabl containing some misinformation. However, neither *The New Grove Dictionary of Music and Musicians* nor *Die Musik in Geschichte und Gegenwart* recognize Rabl.

3. Austrian musicologist Guido Adler, author of numerous important methodological works, taught at the German University of Prague from 1885 to 1895. He later succeeded Eduard Hanslick as professor of musicology at the University of Vienna, retiring in 1927. In his 1929 article, "Musik in Österreich," Adler lists Walter Rabl among the *ganz konservativ* composers such as Felix Weingartner and Max Oberleitner; see *Studien zur Musikwissenschaft* 16 (1929): 30. Rabl's transcriptions of four-part graduals by Heinrich Isaac, originally published by Artaria in 1898, can be found in *Denkmäler der Tonkunst in Österreich*, vols. 10 and 32 (Graz: Akademische Druck- und Verlagsanstalt, 1959).

4. See Richard Heuberger, *Erinnerungen an Johannes Brahms: Tagebuchnotizen aus den Jahren 1875 bis Alfred von Ehrmann 1897* (Tutzing: Hans Schneider, 1976) and *Johannes Brahms: Weg, Werk und Welt* (Leipzig: Breitkopf und Hartel, 1933).

5. Max Kalbeck, *Johannes Brahms* (Berlin: Deutsche Brahms-Gesellschaft, 1914), 4:508–9. See also Malcolm MacDonald, "A Sense of the Past," in *Brahms* (New York: Schirmer Books, 1990), 143–56 and Otto Biba, "New Light on the Brahms *Nachlass*," in *Brahms 2: Biographical, Documentary and Analytical Studies*, ed. Michael Musgrave (Cambridge: Cambridge University Press, 1987), 39–47.

6. For a list of composers recommended to Simrock by Brahms, see Kurt Stephenson, ed., *Johannes Brahms und Fritz Simrock: Weg einer Freundschaft* (Hamburg: J. J. Augustin, 1961), 32. See also Walter Frisch, ed., "Memoirs," in *Brahms and His World* (Princeton: Princeton University Press, 1990), 163–207. This section contains descriptions of Brahms the teacher written by Alexander von Zemlinsky and Gustav Jenner.

7. Eduard Hanslick, *Memories and Letters*, trans. Susan Gillespie (Princeton: Princeton University Press, 1990), 27, as quoted in Frisch, 181.

8. "Falls in Berlin Geld für mich liegt, kann es in den Reichskeller kommen, die Englische Erbschaft reicht noch—trotzdem ich die Preisarbeiten königlich protegiere. Diese sollen am 11ten Dezember bereits alle vorgeführt sein, und dann abgestimmt werden. Das Beste ist jedenfalls ein Pianofortequartett mit Klarinette. Es soll von Rabl, einem Schüler Nawratils, sein. Ich kenne den jungen Mann und seine Sache wenig, da er mir persönlich nicht sympathisch war. Natürlich behalte ich ihn und sein Stück jetzt im Auge" (letter #929 in Max Kalbeck, *Johannes Brahms: Briefe an Fritz Simrock*, vol. 4 [Tutzing: Verlegt bei Hans Schneider, 1974]). Friedrich August (Fritz) Simrock (1837–1901), the third generation director of the Simrock family publishing house, was a close friend and confidant of Brahms, so close, in fact, that Brahms's last will, the so-called Ischl Testament, was written in the form of a letter to him; see Walther Ottendorff-Simrock, *Das Haus Simrock: ein Beitrag zur Geschichte der Kulturtragenden Familien des Rheinlandes* (Ratingen: A. Henn, 1954) and Stephenson, 1–36.

9. Eusebius Mandyczewski (1857–1929) was, beginning in 1887, chief archivist of the Gesellschaft der Musikfreunde and, beginning in 1897, professor of music history at the Hochschule für Musik in Vienna. He was also a close friend and factotum of Brahms during the composer's old age. Mandyczewski's name is scrawled on the title page of the copy of Rabl's quartet (cataloged as part of the Brahms *Nachlass* at the Gesellschaft) used for the present edition. His edition of the complete piano oeuvre of Brahms is still printed by G. Schirmer today.

10. Joseph Miroslav Weber was *Konzertmeister* in Munich at the time of the competition. Simrock never published his prize-winning piece and the original appears to be lost.

Composer and conductor Alexander von Zemlinsky is perhaps best remembered today as the teacher of Arnold Schoenberg and Alban Berg. A prolific and successful composer (his six operas received considerable acclaim throughout the German speaking world), Zemlinsky saw his Trio, op. 3, published by Simrock in 1897; see *Verzeichnis des Musikalien-Verlages N. Simrock* (Berlin: Simrock, 1897). The trio was republished by Musica Rara in 1980.

11. MacDonald, 410.

12. "Über unsern Preiskomponisten Walter Rabl werde ich immer Erfreulicheres melden. Ein ganzer Stoß Sachen von ihm liegt bei mir. Er selbst kommt der Tage zum Fest, ist im Begriff, in Prag seinen Doktor zu machen. Die Abstimmung ist am 22sten; ich glaube, daß er den ersten Preis kriegt—das ist aber ganz Nebensache. Alles wird bestens besorgt von Deinem J. B." (letter #930 in Kalbeck).

13. "Nebenbei hat Herr Rabl also auch den ersten Preis gekriegt. Dich angehend, wird alles bestens besorgt, und er ist sehr glücklich darüber" (letter #932 in Kalbeck).

14. "Du hast ja ein unglaubliches Verlangen nach Novitäten! Das Quartett von Rabl und das Trio von Zemlinsky gehören Dir. Bei beiden kann ich eben auch den Menschen und das Talent empfehlen. Wenn Rabl zögert, Dir das Quartett zu schicken, so ist das wohl meine Schuld, er meint warten zu sollen, bis er Gleichwertiges beilegen oder gleich folgen lassen kann" (letter #933 in Kalbeck).

15. Eccarius-Sieber, 194.

16. D. Rahter [firm], *Verlags-Verzeichnis D. Rahter, Leipzig: 1879–1909* (Leipzig: D. Rahter, 1910). At the turn of the century, Rahter was publishing conservative composers like Georg Henschel, Karl Reinecke, and Walter Rabl, as well as modern composers like Richard Strauss.

17. Marcel Prawy, *Die Wiener Oper* (Vienna: Verlag Fritz Molden, 1969), 81. A picture of the winsome Lucille Marcel appears in *The New Grove Dictionary of Music and Musicians*, s.v. "Weingartner, (Paul) Felix." Considering the frequency of Hermine Rabl von Kriesten's appearance at the Hofoper in 1910 and 1911 and the important roles she sang, Frau Rabl is conspicuously absent in Marcel Prawy's work. She is also missing from *The New Grove Dictionary of Opera*.

18. "Weiteren Kreisen der musikalischen Welt hat sich der Kapellmeister und Komponist Dr. Walter Rabl durch die Aufführungen seiner romantischen Märchenoper *Liane* bekannt gemacht, durch ein Werk, das, seiner ganzen Anlage und Fassung nach der Wagnerischen Kunstrichtung angehörend, bei

xiii

seinem Erscheinen umsomehr auffallen mußte, als Walter Rabl, der preisgekrönte Autor eines schönen Klarinetten-Quartettes, vorher zu der Brahmspartei gehörig betrachtet wurde" (Eccarius-Sieber, 193).

19. Eccarius-Sieber, 193–95.

20. "Der Komponist beherrscht das moderne Orchester vollständig: besondere Aufmerksamkeit schien mir den Streichinstrumenten zugewandt"; *Elsässer Volksbote* (Strasbourg), 19 March 1903.

21. "Fraglos hat man es in Walter Rabl mit einem schaffenden Tonkünstler zu tun, der fest den auf altklassischer Kultur aufgebauten Boden neuzeitiger Kunst betreten hat, sowie deren Technik und Hilfsmittel vollkommen beherrscht"; *Straßburger Post*, 19 March 1903.

22. "Trotz einiger Anlehnungen an das unverkennbare Vorbild Richard Wagner hegen wir die Zuversicht, daß Walter Rabl mit der *Liane* in die Reihe der wenigen Musiker getreten ist, auf welche die Zukunft ihre Hoffnung gründet"; *Straßburger Zeitung*, 19 March 1903.

23. "Wir stehen hier tatsächlich vor einem selten schönen Werke. Die Tonsprache ist eine so edle, so tiefempfundene, daß sie keiner geringeren, als der wunderbaren Tonsprache Richard Wagners gleichkommt. . . . Nirgends auch nur das leiseste Andeuten einer trivialen Wendung!"; "Kunst, Wissenschaft und Literatur," *Straßburger Neuste Nachrichten*, 19 March 1903.

24. "Der Erfolg des Werkes war—nach der Stimmung im Publikum zu schließen—ein unbestreitbar großer. Wir glauben, daß sich die *Liane* allein in ihrer Eigenschaft als dekoratives Bühnenwerk dauernd auf dem Repertoire unserer Oper halten wird," newspaper (Düsseldorf), 8 February 1905.

25. "So begegnen wir dem ehemaligen Quartettkomponisten und Beherrscher des Brahmsschen Stiles nun auch unter den Operndichtern wieder"; Eccarius-Sieber, 194.

26. "Als Komponist hat er lange vor dem Ausbruch des Ersten Weltkrieges aufgehört, zu schreiben. Sein letztes Werk, eine Oper (*Liane* nach einem hübschen, romantischen Buch eines feinsinnigen Dresdner Lyrikers, Wilhelm Eberhard Ernst), wurde von der Kritik nach der Uraufführung, wie er mir einmal erzählte, seiner Ansicht nach mit Recht dahin gekennzeichnet, daß stilistische Anklänge an Wagner unverkennbar seien. Er zog daraus in (übertriebener?) Selbstkritik den Schluß, daß ihm die kompositorischen Schöpferkräfte fehlten und es daher richtig sei, auf weitere Versuche in diesem Feld zu verzichten. Vielleicht lag es auch daran, daß er das Gefühl hatte, der Brahms'schen Tradition untreu geworden und ins Lager der damals allzu zahlreichen Wagner-Epigonen übergegangen zu sein." Dr. Kurt Rabl to the editors, 13 May 1986. Most of our information about Walter Rabl's last two decades comes from correspondence and conversations with his son, Dr. Kurt Rabl.

27. "Er war ein gottbegnadeter Pianist, der von sehr vielen, zu seiner Zeit berühmten Liedinterpreten (Maria Ivogün, Lauriz Melchior, Heinrich Knothe, Heinrich Schlusnus u. v. a. m. [und viele andere mehr]) als Klavierbegleiter hochgeschätzt und gesucht war. Ich selbst verdanke meine größten, bis heute unverblaßten Jugendeindrücke Liederabenden, bei denen er Kompositionen von Brahms, Schubert (Winterreise!) oder Wolf am Klavier begleitete." Dr. Kurt Rabl to the editors, 13 May 1986.

28. José Subira y Puig, *Historia y Anecdotario del Teatro Real* (Madrid: Ed. Plus-Ultra, 1949), 604–47.

29. "Als Opern- und Konzertchef der Stadt hat er sich vor allem um die Durchsetzung Bruckners und der damaligen neuromantischen Modern (Schreker, Korngold) verdient gemacht." Dr. Kurt Rabl to the editors, 13 May 1986.

30. *Städtisches Orchester Magdeburg* (Magdeburg: Rat der Stadt Magdeburg, 1987), 20–21.

31. MacDonald, 29.

32. The publisher stresses that "The *Fantasiestücke*, nos. 1–8, constitutes a **unified whole.** The division into two volumes was solely for practical reasons" (Die *Fantasiestücke* No. 1–8 bilden ein **zusammenhängendes Ganzes.** Die Eintheilung in 2 Hefte erfolgte lediglich aus praktischen Gründen). The boldface type is found in the original.

Plate 1. Rabl as a young man. Reproduced from A. Eccarius-Sieber, *Monographien Moderner Musiker: 20 Biographien zeitgenossischer Tonsetzer mit Portraits*, vol. 2 (Leipzig: C. F. Kahnt Nachfolger, 1907).

Plate 2. Title page of the Quartet for Violin, Clarinet (or Viola), Violoncello, and Piano, op. 1 (Berlin: Simrock, 1907). (Courtesy of Gesellschaft der Musikfreunde, Vienna)

Quartet, Op. 1

I

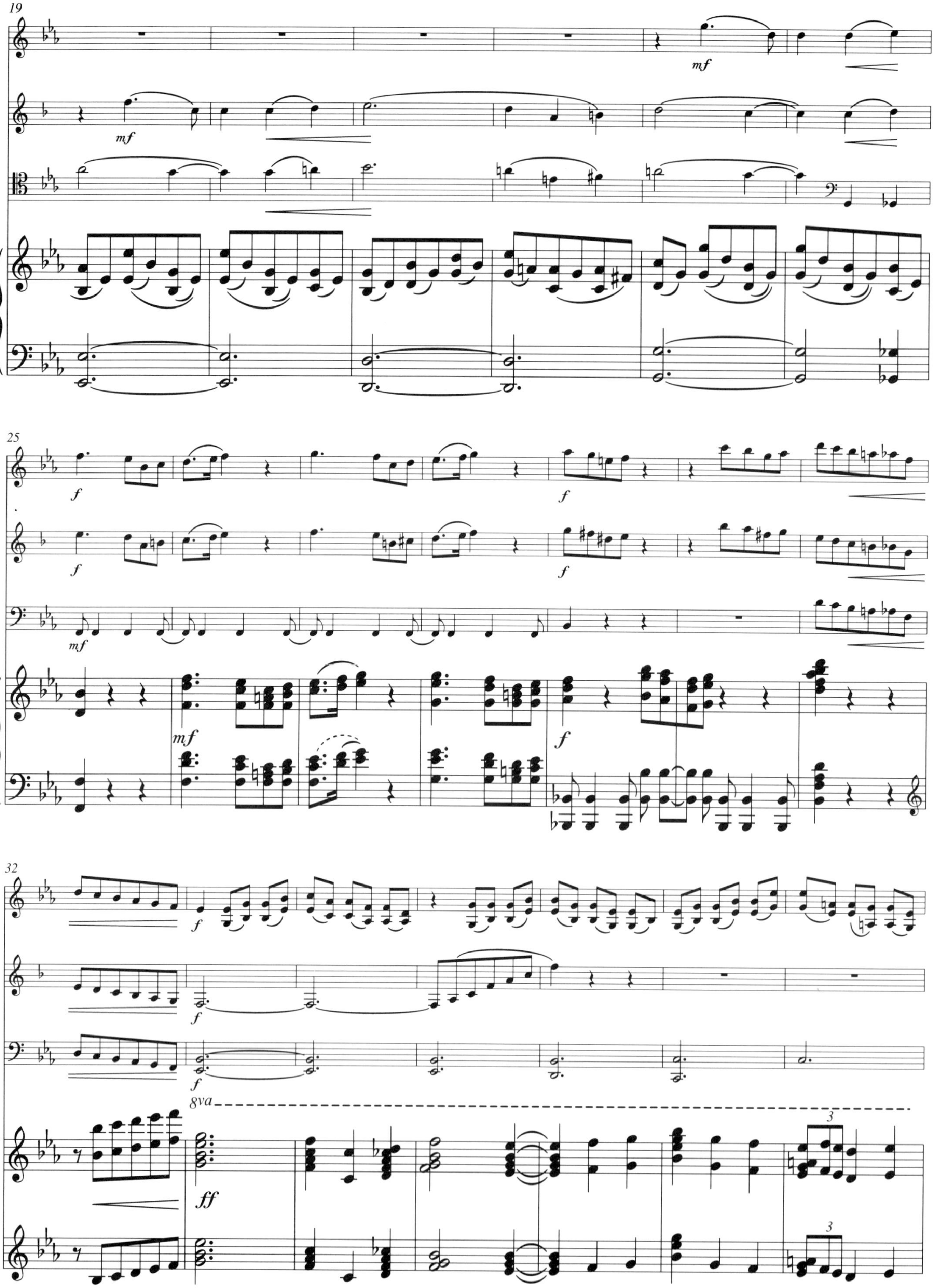
19
mf
25
f
32
8va
ff
3

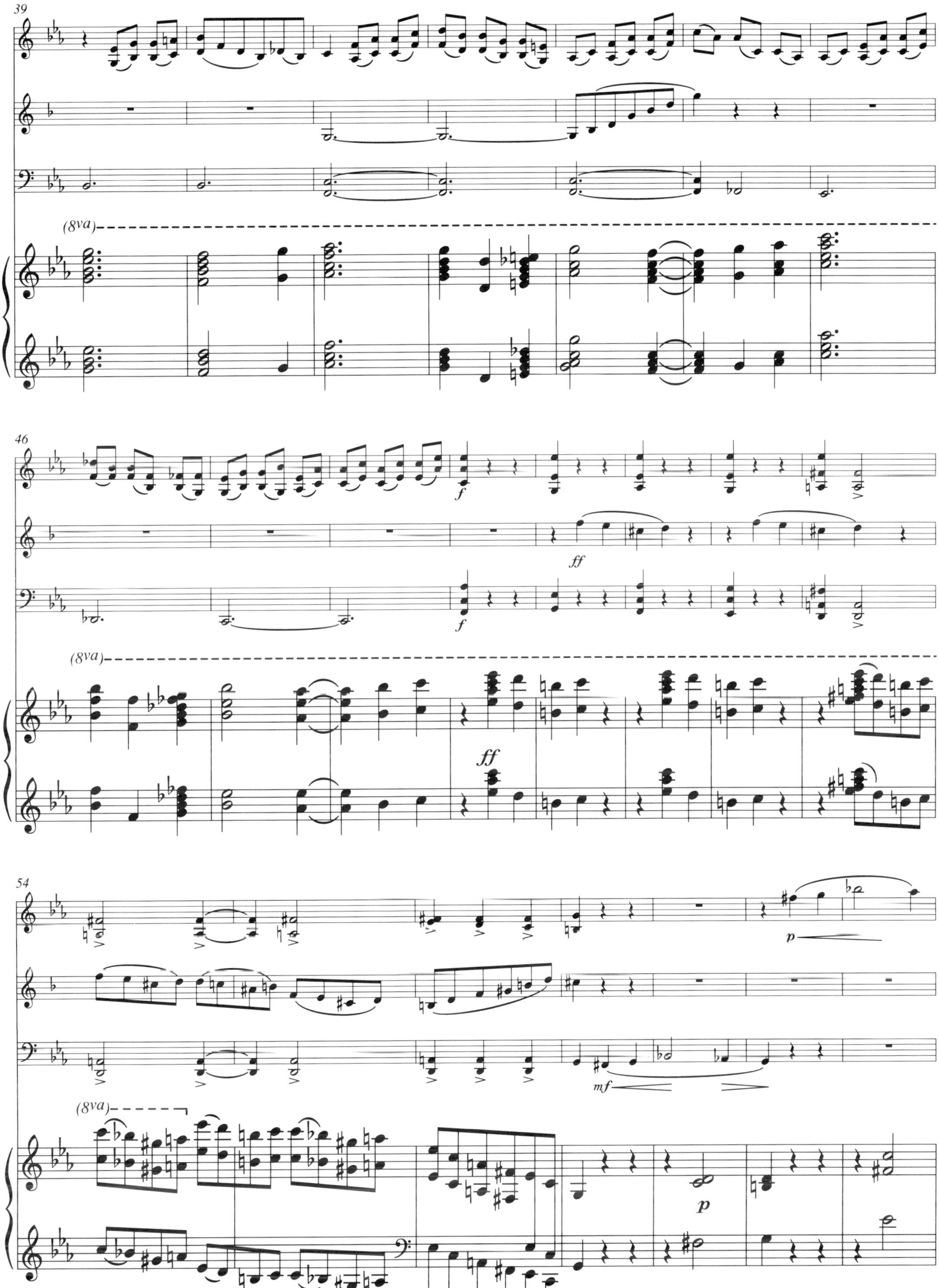
39
(8va)
46
f
ff
(8va)
54
p
mf
(8va)

61
pizz.
arco
p
pp leggiero
70
8va
pp
79
rit.
a tempo
pizz.
arco
p a tempo

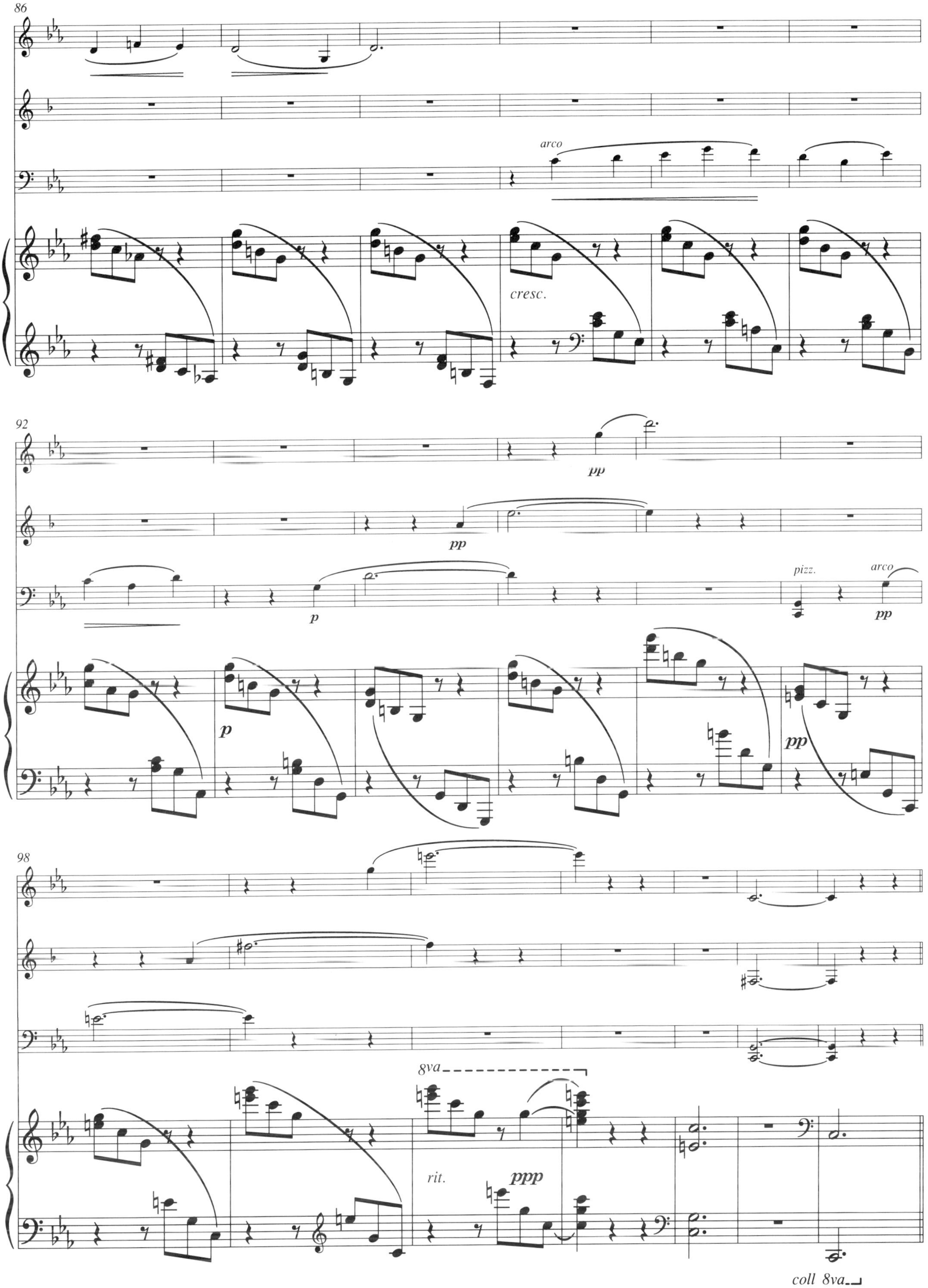

86
arco
cresc.
92
pp
pp
p
pizz.
arco
pp
p
pp
98
8va
rit.
ppp
coll 8va

105
Vivo
ff
Vivo
ff
111
ff
8va
117
f con fuoco
con fuoco
f
8va
8va

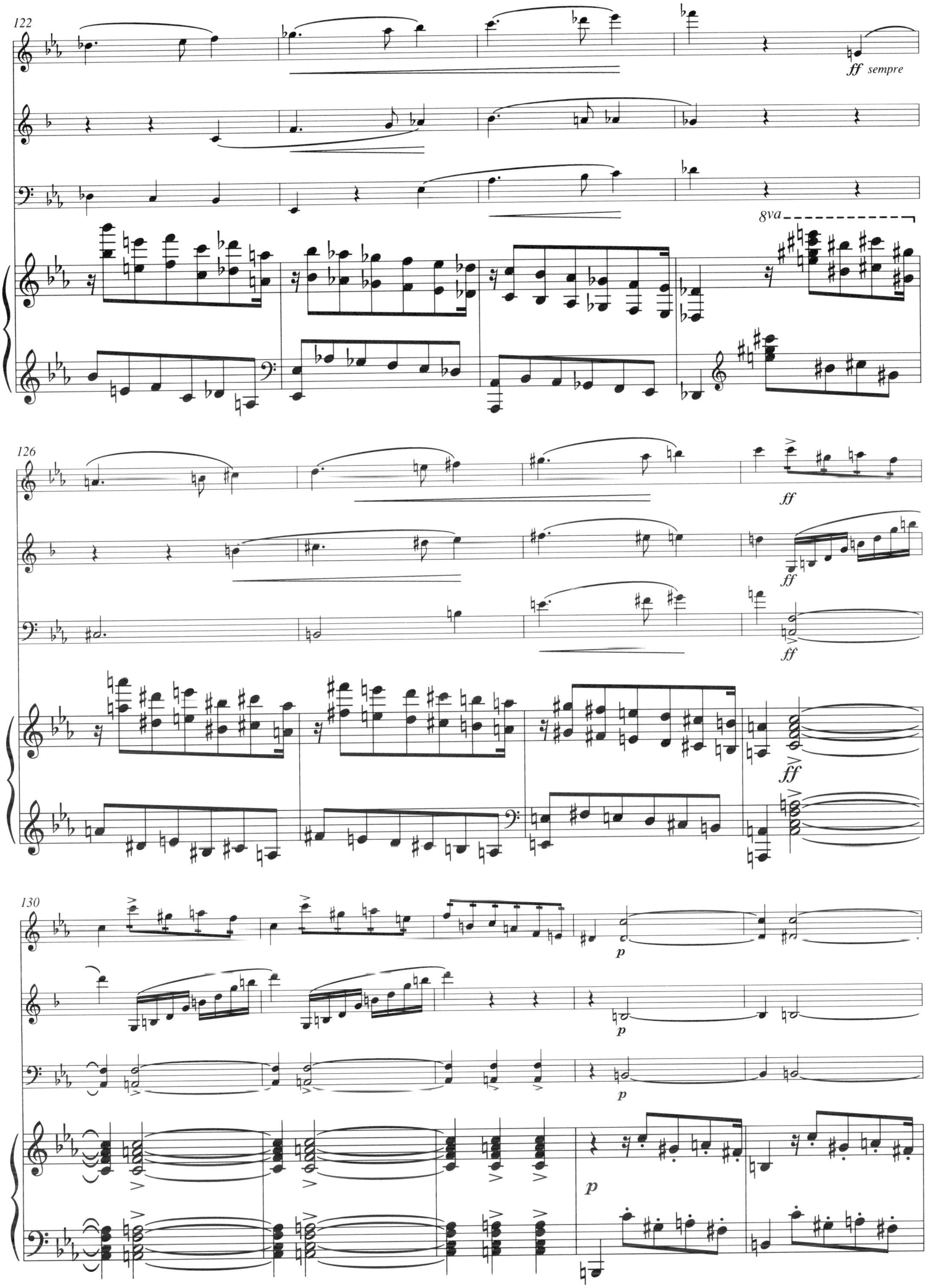
122
ff sempre
8va
126
ff
ff
ff
ff
130
p
p
p
p

135
rit.
Tempo I
rit.
p espress.
rit.
p tranquillo ed espress.
Tempo I
tranquillo
rit.
p
140
p espress.
mf espress.
mf espress.
146
mf espress.
f
p
f
mf
p
f

154
p
pp
mf
p
f
p
p espress.
p
3
p cantando
162
3
sim.
169
p espress.
p
sim.
mf
f

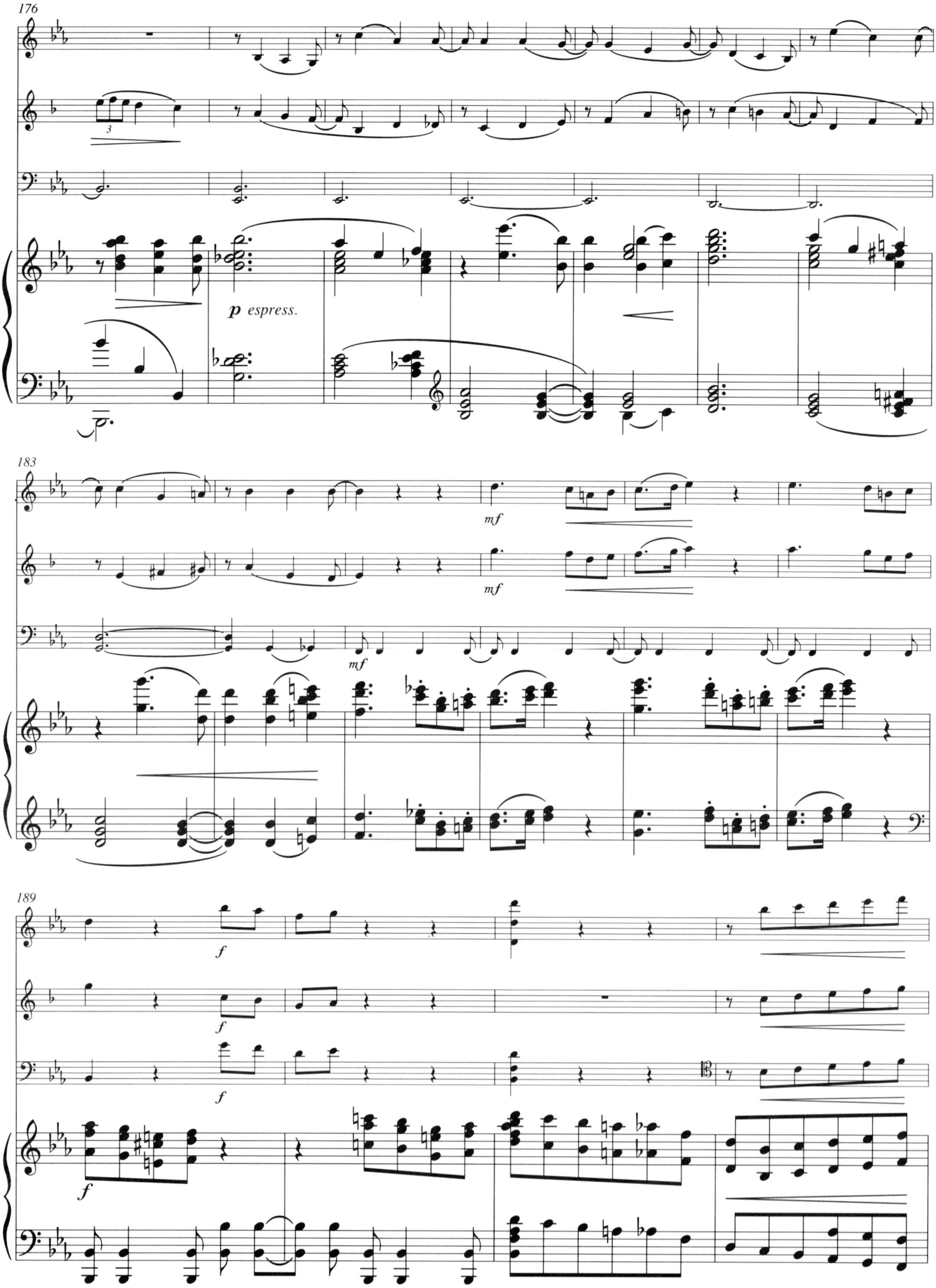
176
p espress.
183
mf
mf
mf
189
f
f
f
f

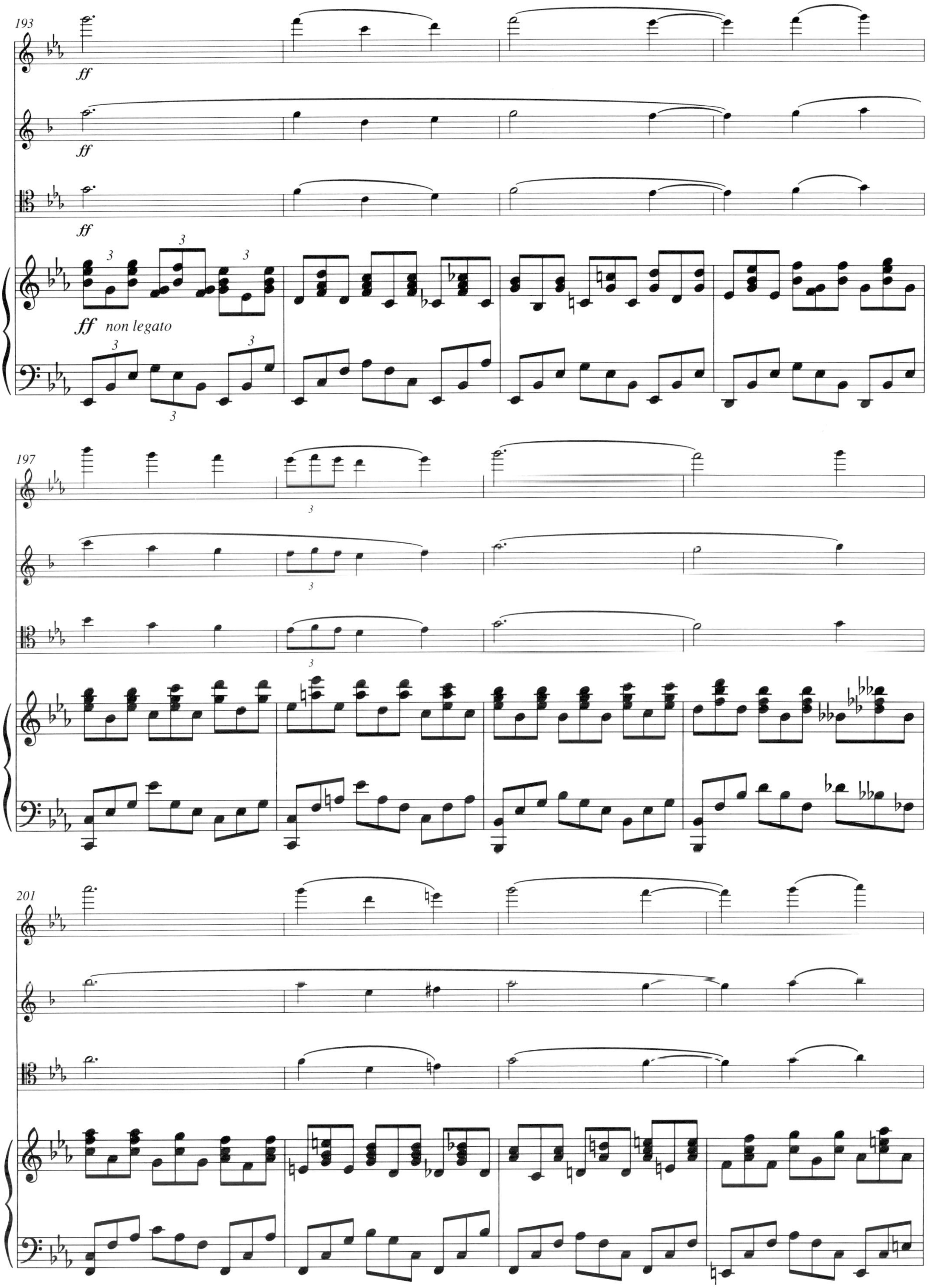
193
ff
ff
ff
ff non legato
197
201

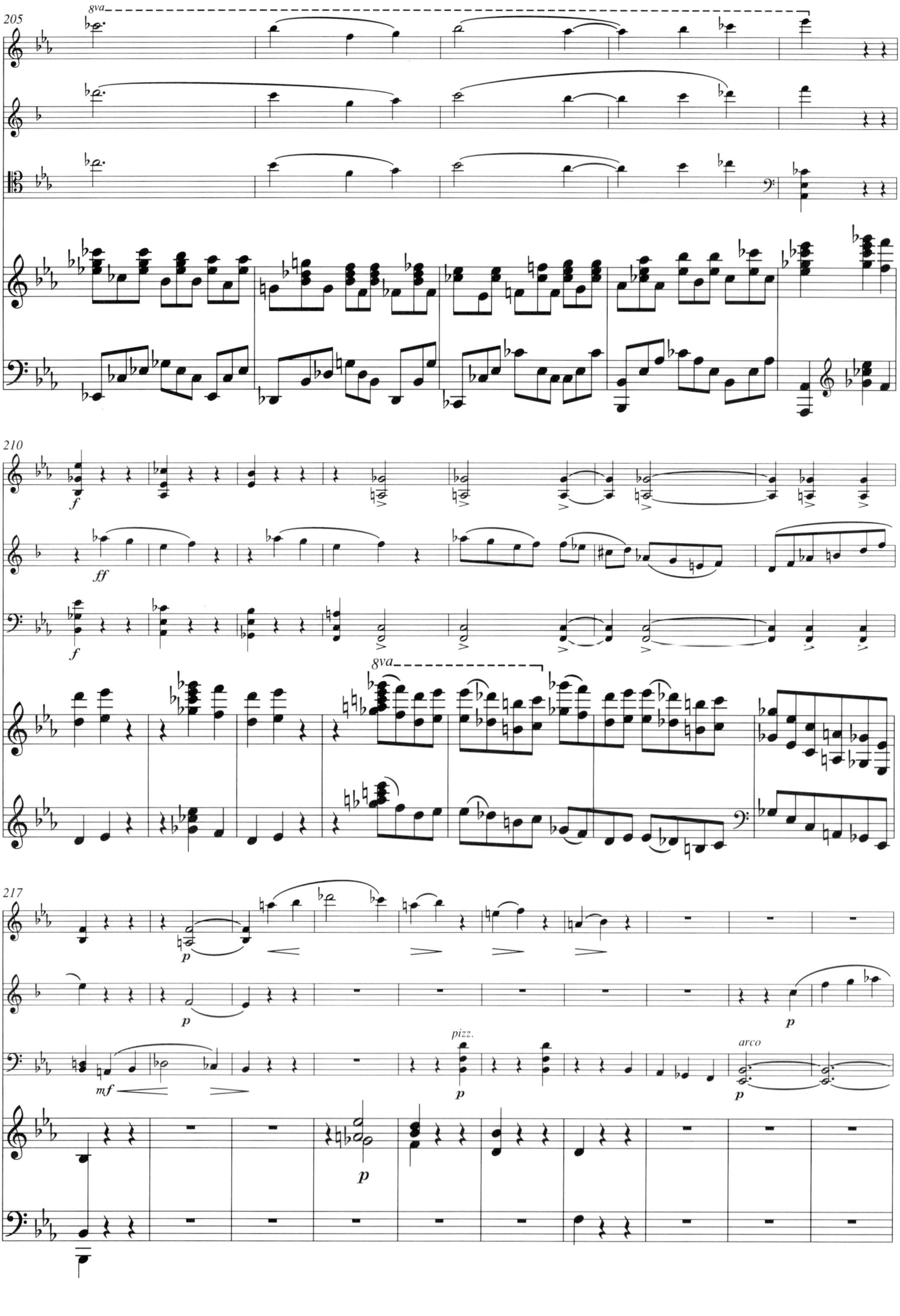
205
8va
210
f
ff
f
8va
217
p
mf
pizz.
p
arco
p
p

227
pp leggiero
230
rit.
a tempo
pp
p
8va
rit.
p a tempo
243
sul G
sim.

14

15

281
ff
ff
ff
287
8va
coll 8va
292
fff largamente
fff largamente
fff largamente
(8va)
fff largamente
(coll 8va)

17

II

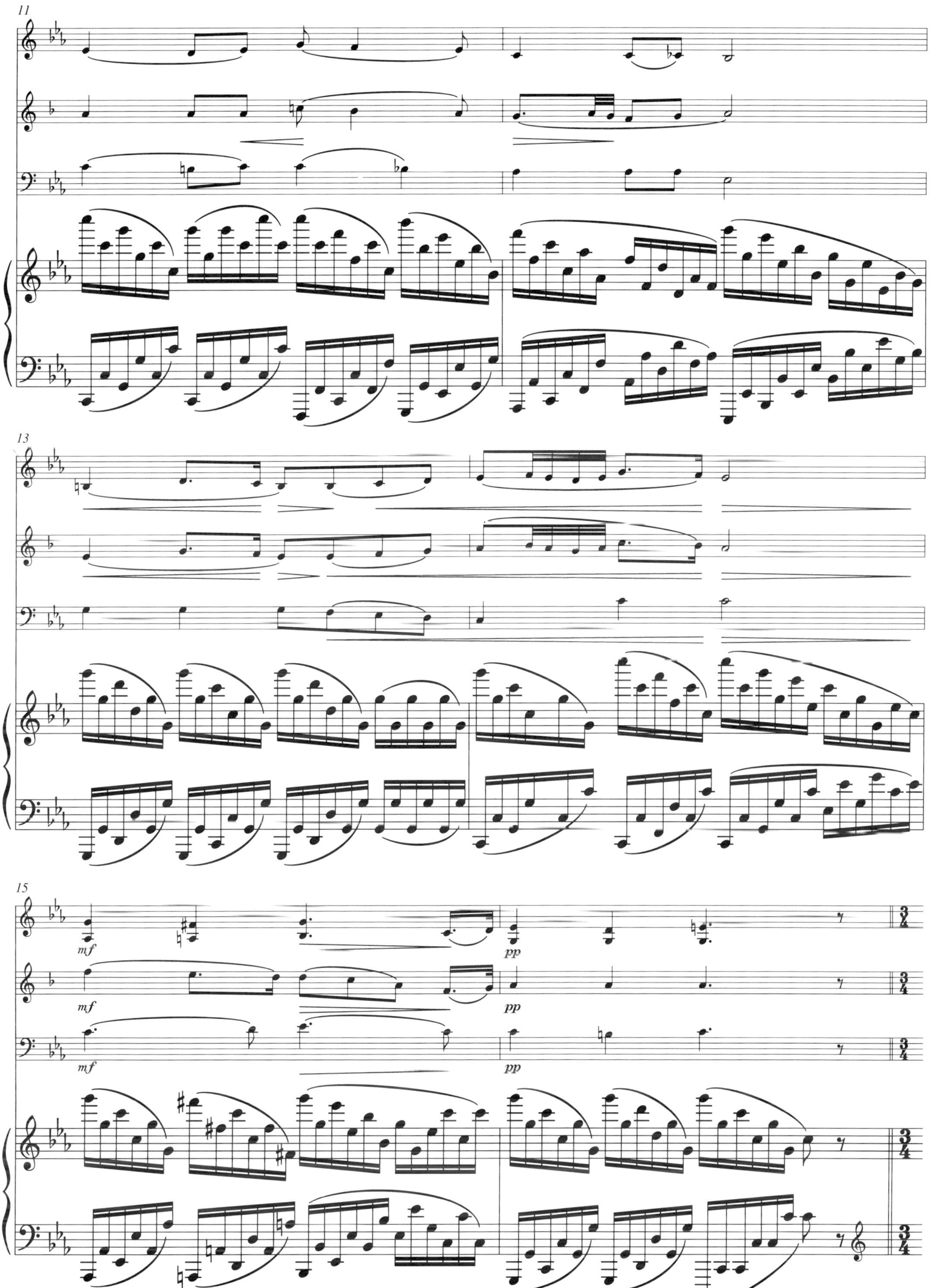
11
13
15
mf
pp
mf
pp
mf
pp

17
Allegro vivace M.M. ♩ = 120
pizz.
arco
Allegro vivace M.M. ♩ = 120
21
arco
pizz.
8va
25
pizz.
arco
scherzando
8va
scherzando

29
arco
f
ff
arco
(8va)
8va
33
Adagio molto e cantabile M.M. ♩ = 32
p con sentimento
pp
p
Adagio molto e cantabile M.M. ♩ = 32
[sim.]
36
p con sentimento

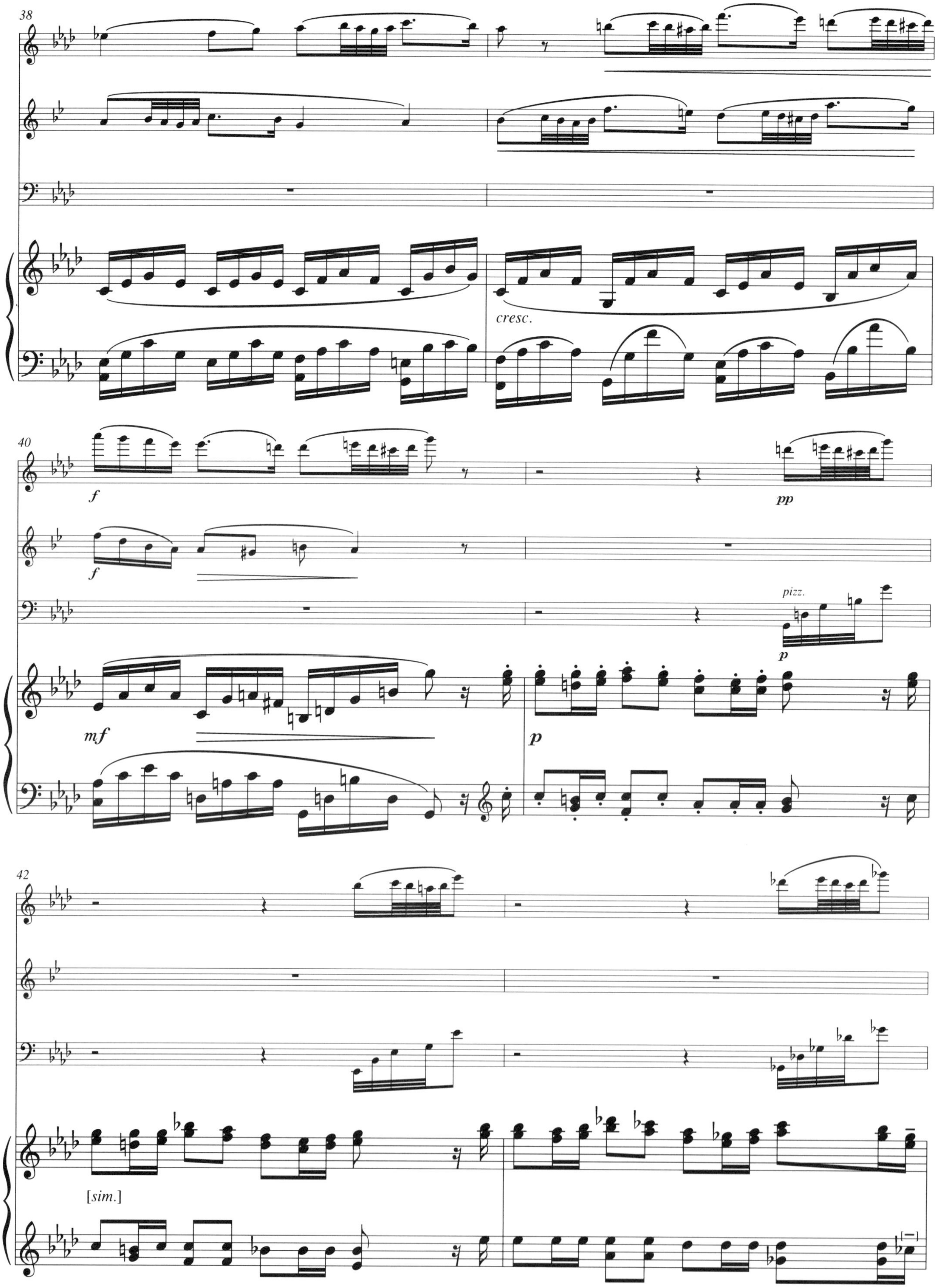
38
cresc.
40
f
f
mf
pp
pizz.
p
p
42
[sim.]

44
rit.
a tempo
a tempo
a tempo
arco
con sentimento
p
rit.
a tempo
46
47
mf
mf
mf
mf

48
5
pp
50
pp
pp
pp
rit.
rit.
rit.
rit.
lento
lento
lento
lento
53
Andante ma non troppo M.M. ♩ = 96
p
Andante ma non troppo M.M. ♩ = 96
p

58
sim.
mf
f
sim.
63
rit.
a tempo vivo
rit.
a tempo vivo
rit.
a tempo vivo
rit.
mf a tempo vivo
68
mf
f

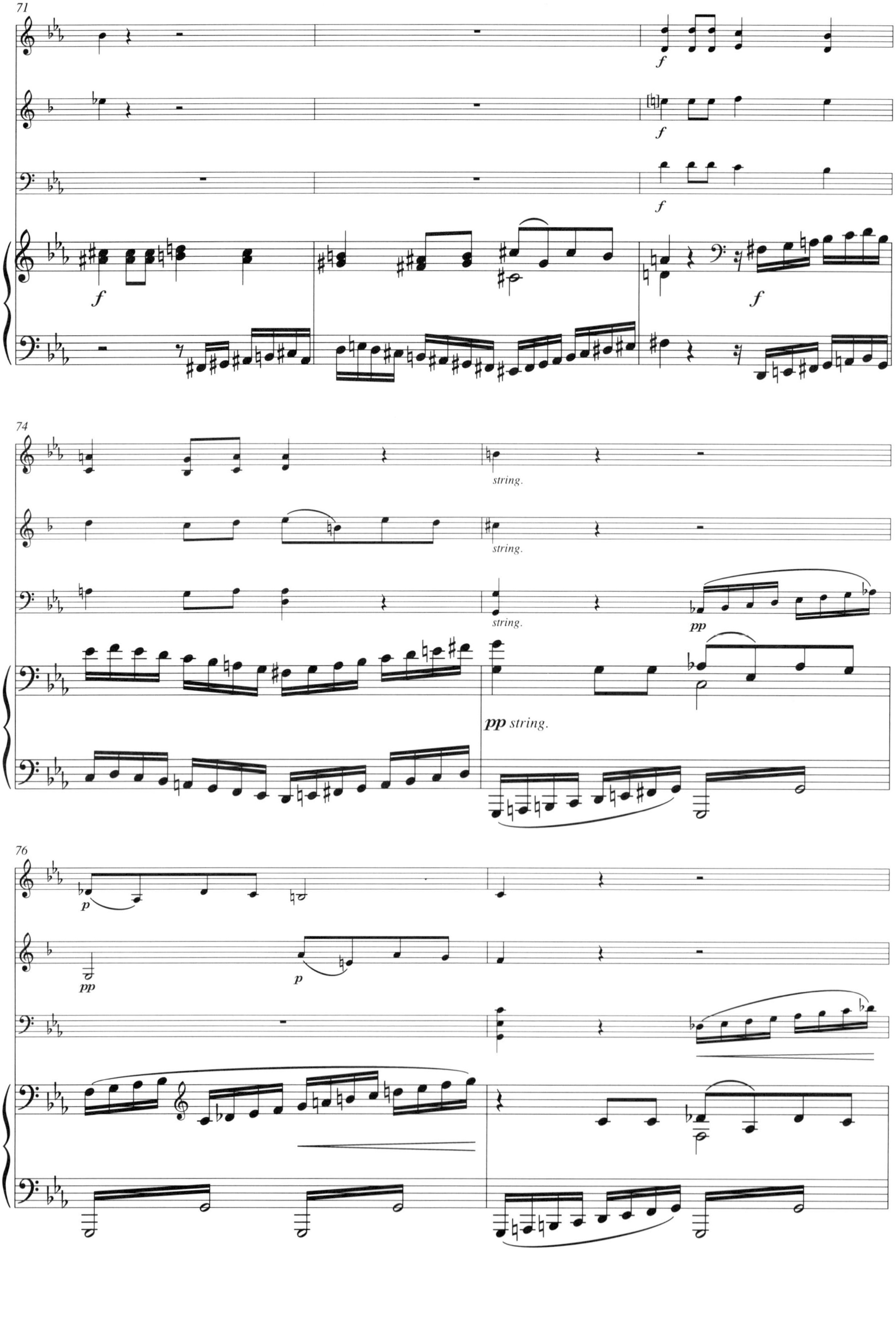
71
f
f
f
f
f
74
string.
string.
string.
pp
pp string.
76
p
pp
p

78
mf più string. e cresc.
mf più string. e cresc.
mf più string. e cresc.
80
83
f con fuoco
ff con fuoco
f con fuoco
ff con fuoco

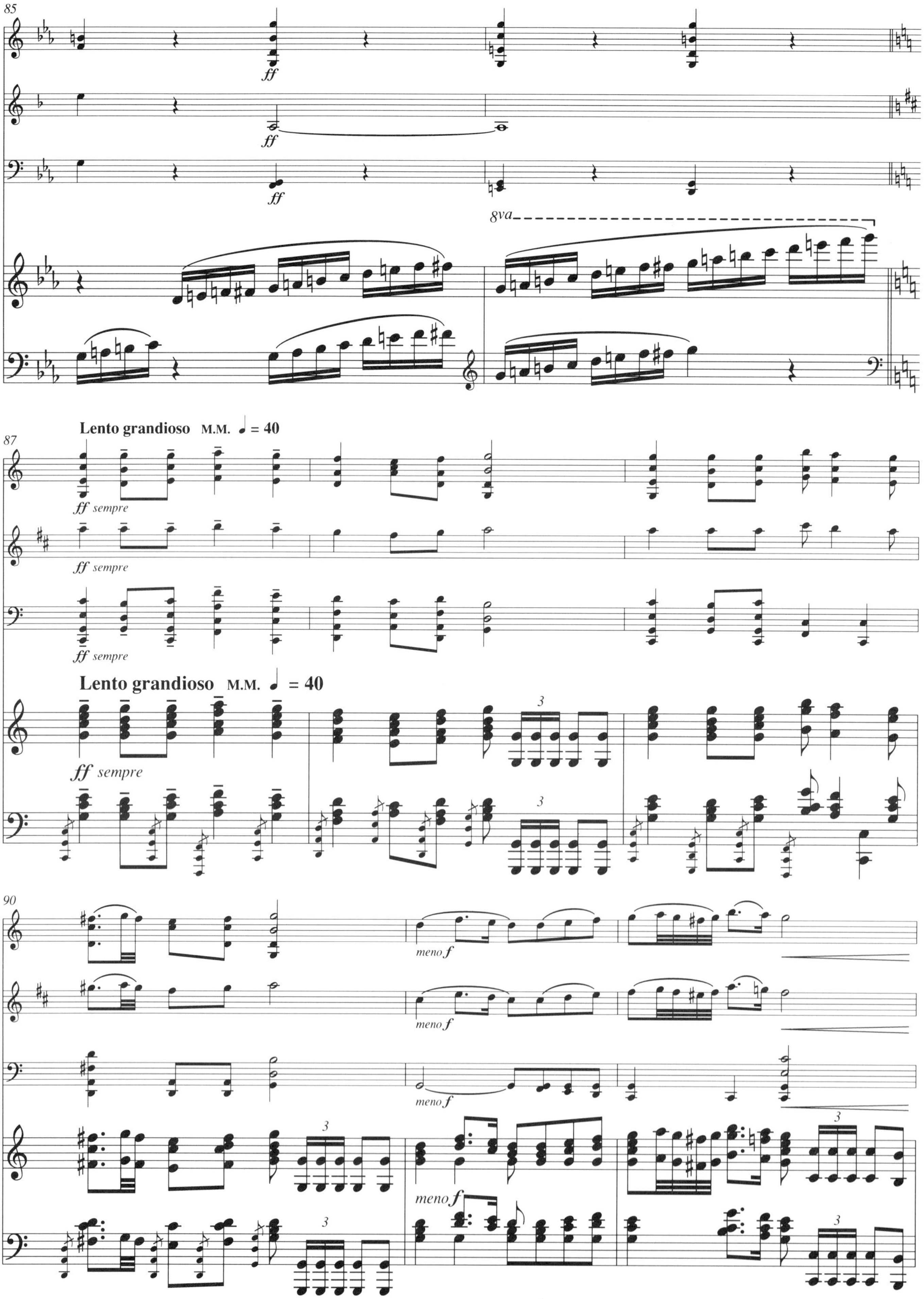
85
ff
8va
87
Lento grandioso M.M. ♩ = 40
ff sempre
3
90
meno f

29

III

31

29
pizz.
arco
pizz.
arco
p
p
33
rit.
sul A
a tempo
Tempo I
pp
rit.
a tempo
pp
rit.
a tempo
arco
pp
espress. assai
8va
8va
Tempo I
rit.
a tempo
come sopra
37
pp
pp

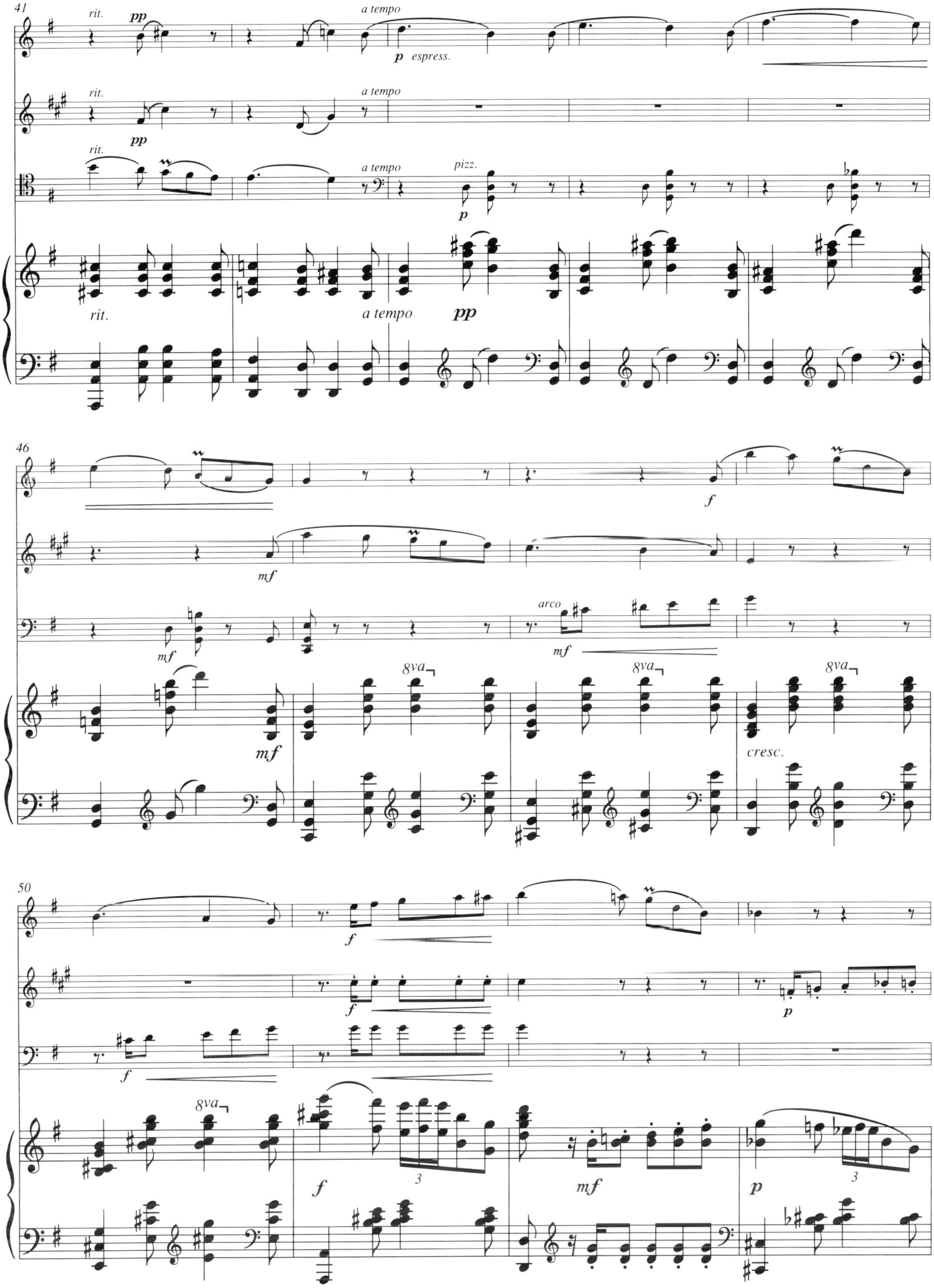
41
rit.
pp
a tempo
p espress.
pizz.
p
46
mf
arco
f
8va
cresc.
50
3
p

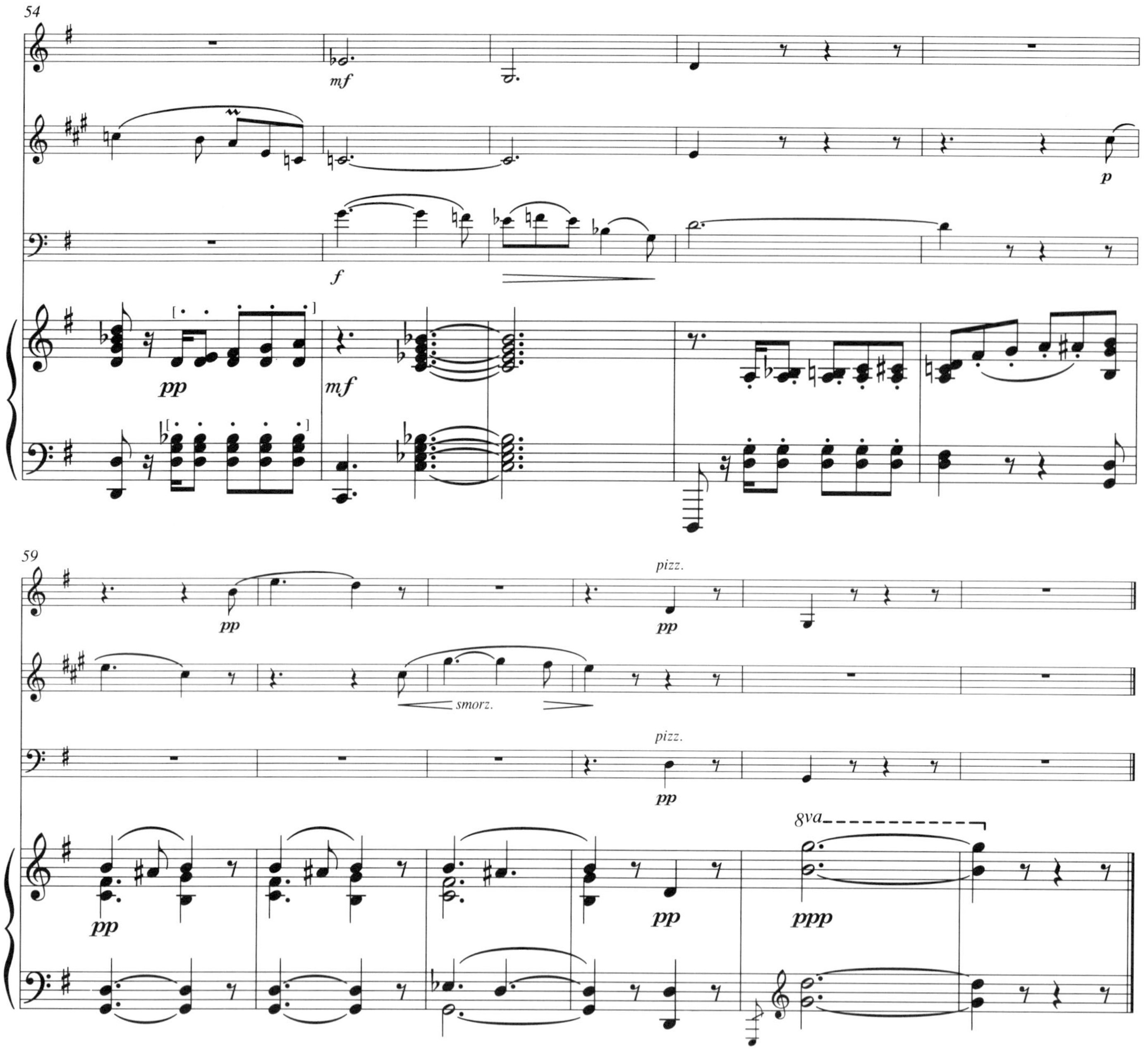
54
mf
pp
f
p
59
pizz.
smorz.
8va
ppp

IV

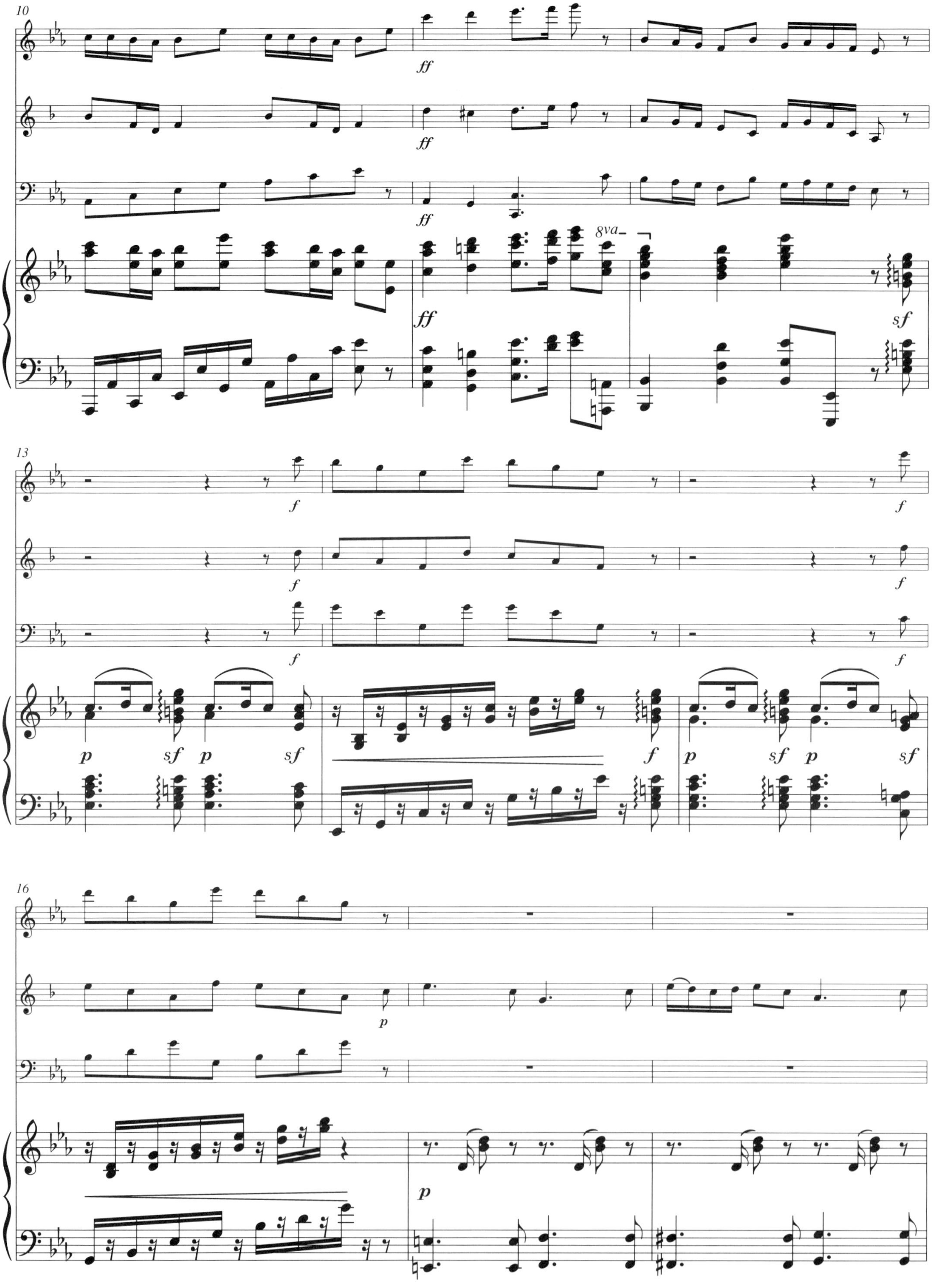
10
ff
ff
ff
ff
8va
sf
13
f
f
f
p
sf
p
sf
f
p
sf
p
sf
f
f
f
16
p
p

37

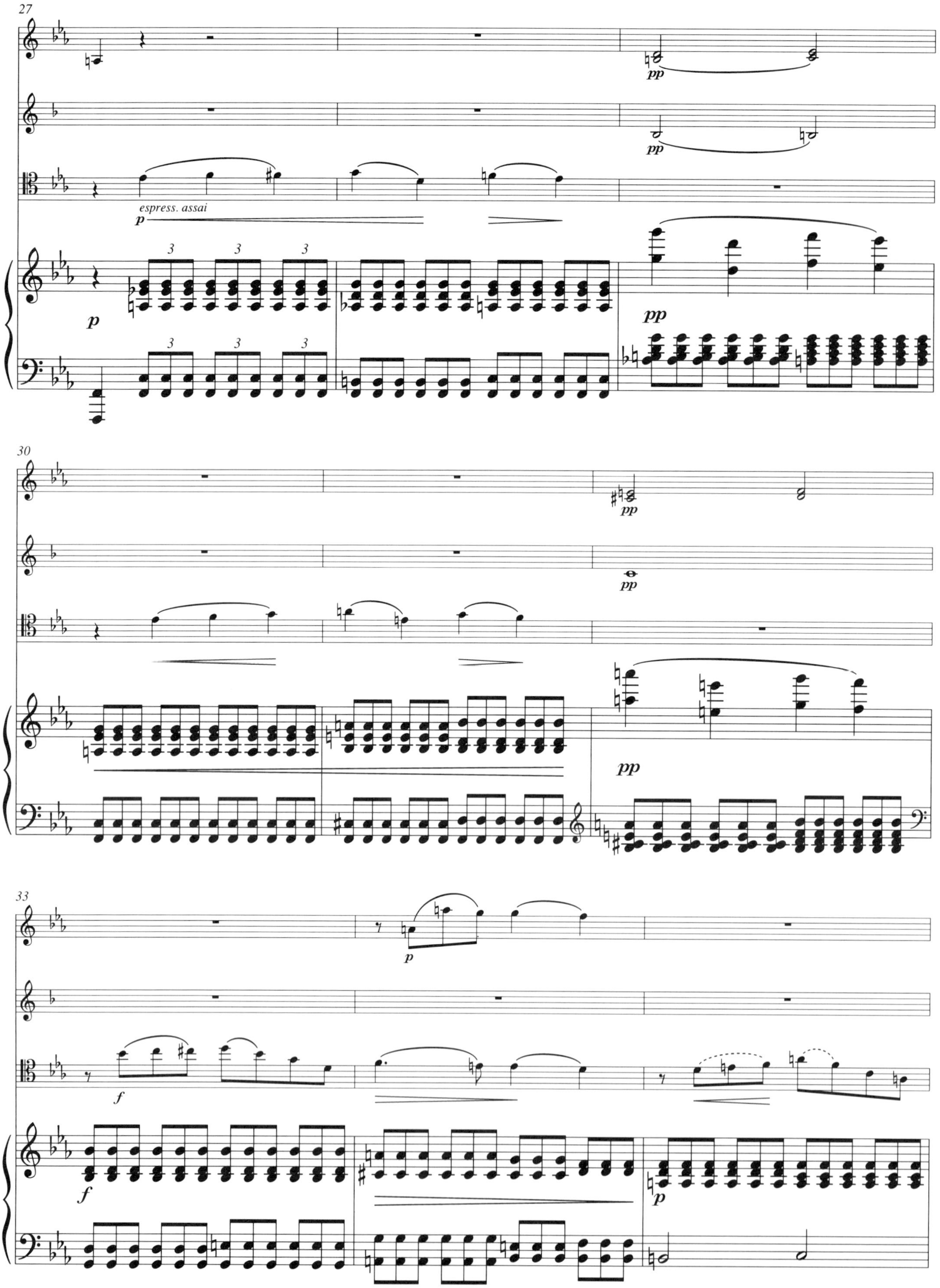
27
pp
pp
espress. assai
p
p
pp
30
pp
pp
pp
33
p
f
f
p

36
p espress. assai
8va
p
39
pp
pizz.
p
(8va)
sempre legato
42
pp
(8va)
arco
p

45
mf
p
mf
mf
p
48
cresc.
f
f
cresc.
51
ff appass.
ff appass.
ff appass.
8va
ff
appass.

41

60
8va
8va
ff
63
ff
ff
ff
(8va)
66
pizz.
mf
pp
mf
pp
pizz.
mf
pp
mf
p
pp
8va
8va
8va
8va
8va
8va

43

44

45

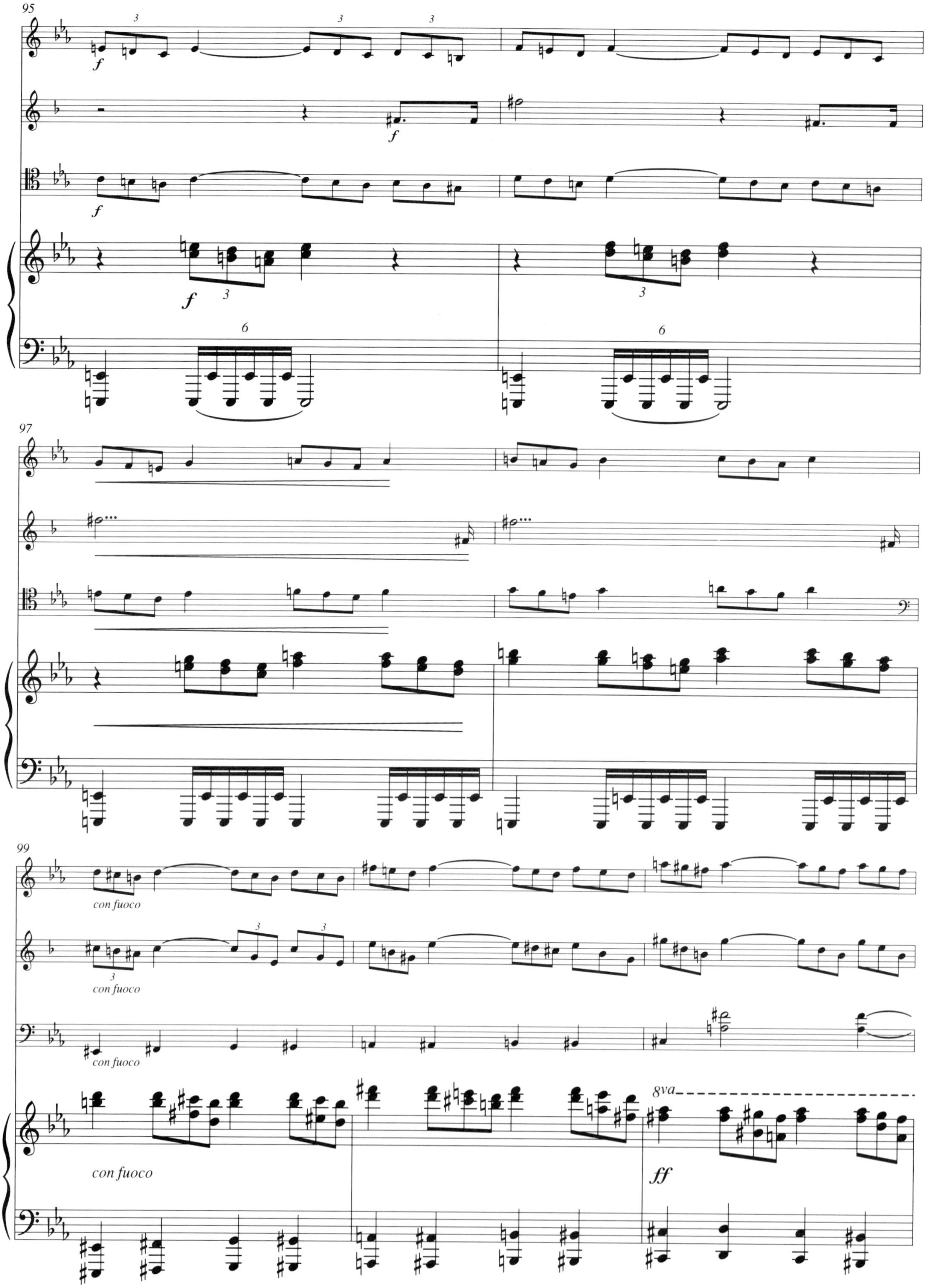
95
97
99
con fuoco
con fuoco
con fuoco
con fuoco
8va

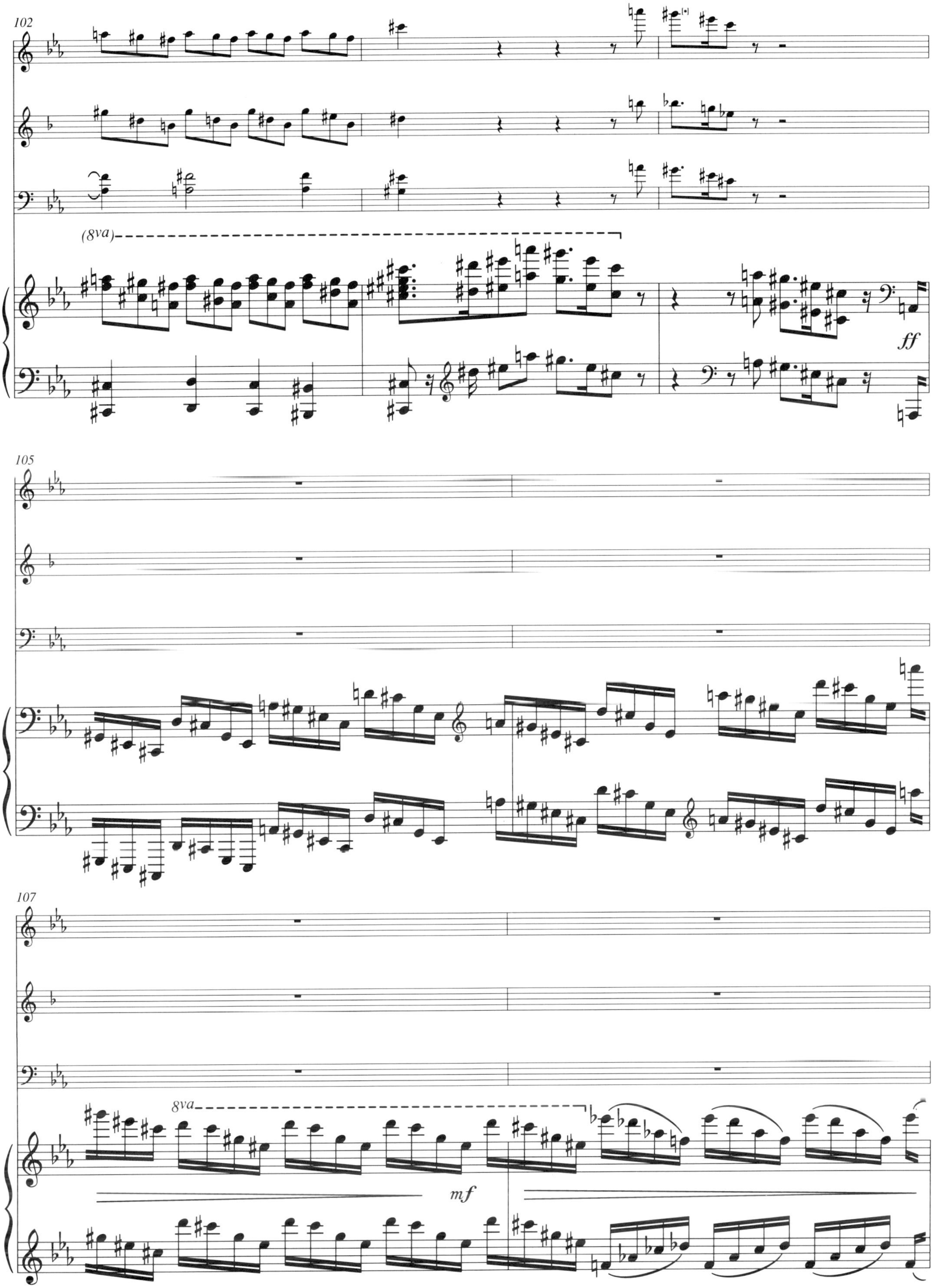
102
(8va)
ff
105
107
8va
mf

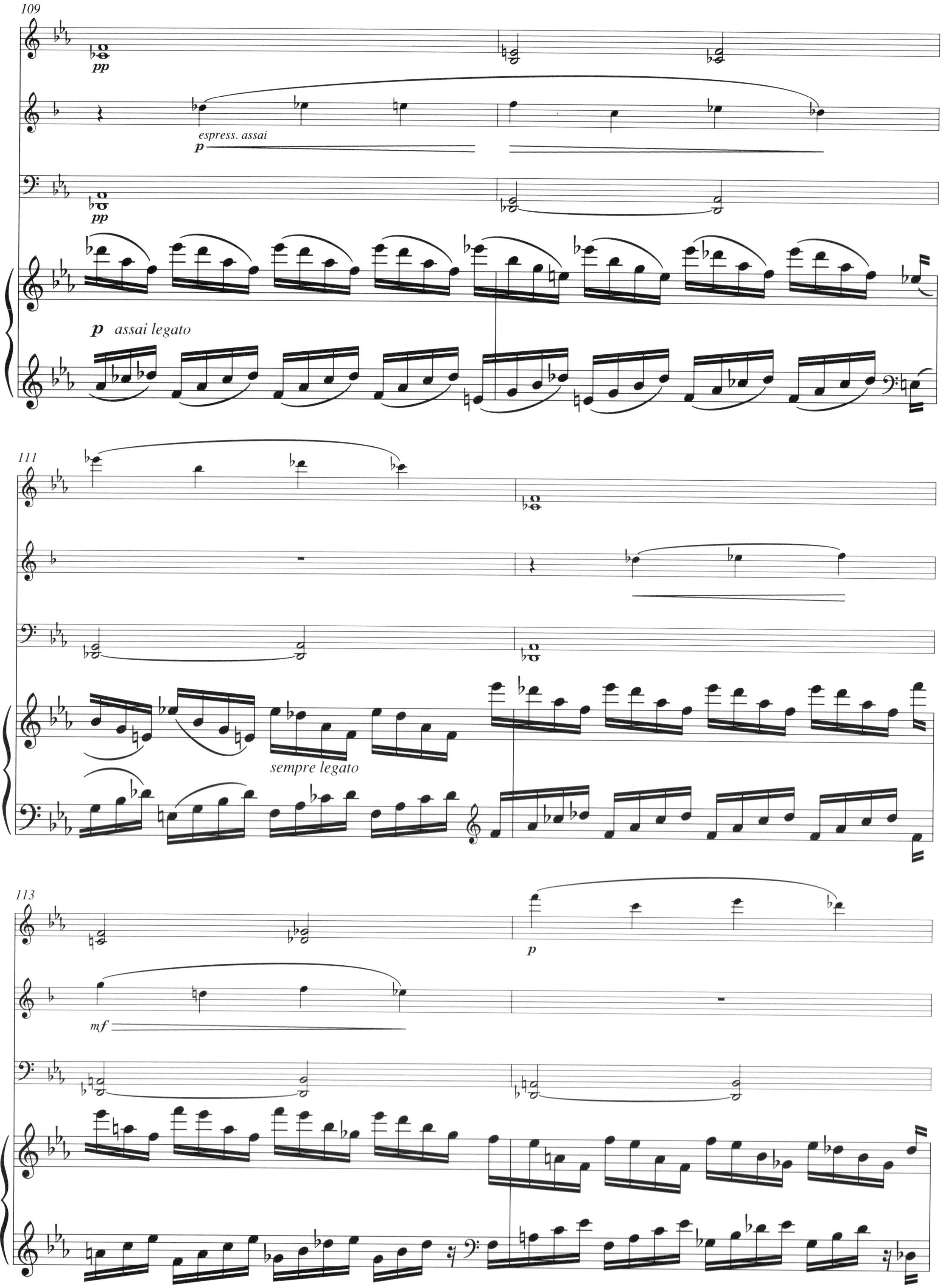
109
pp
espress. assai
p
pp
p assai legato
111
sempre legato
113
p
mf

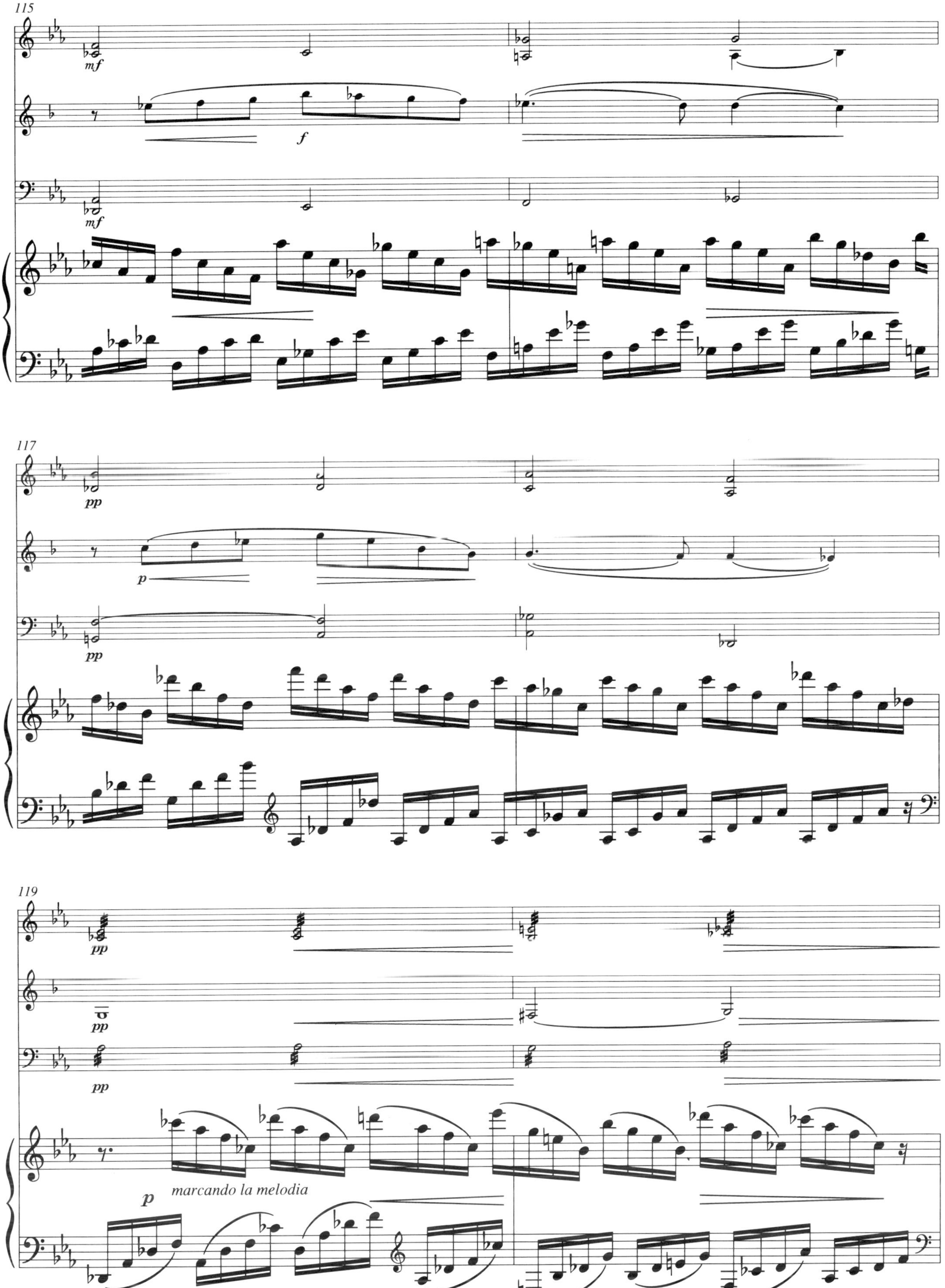
115
mf
f
mf
117
pp
p
pp
119
pp
pp
pp
marcando la melodia
p

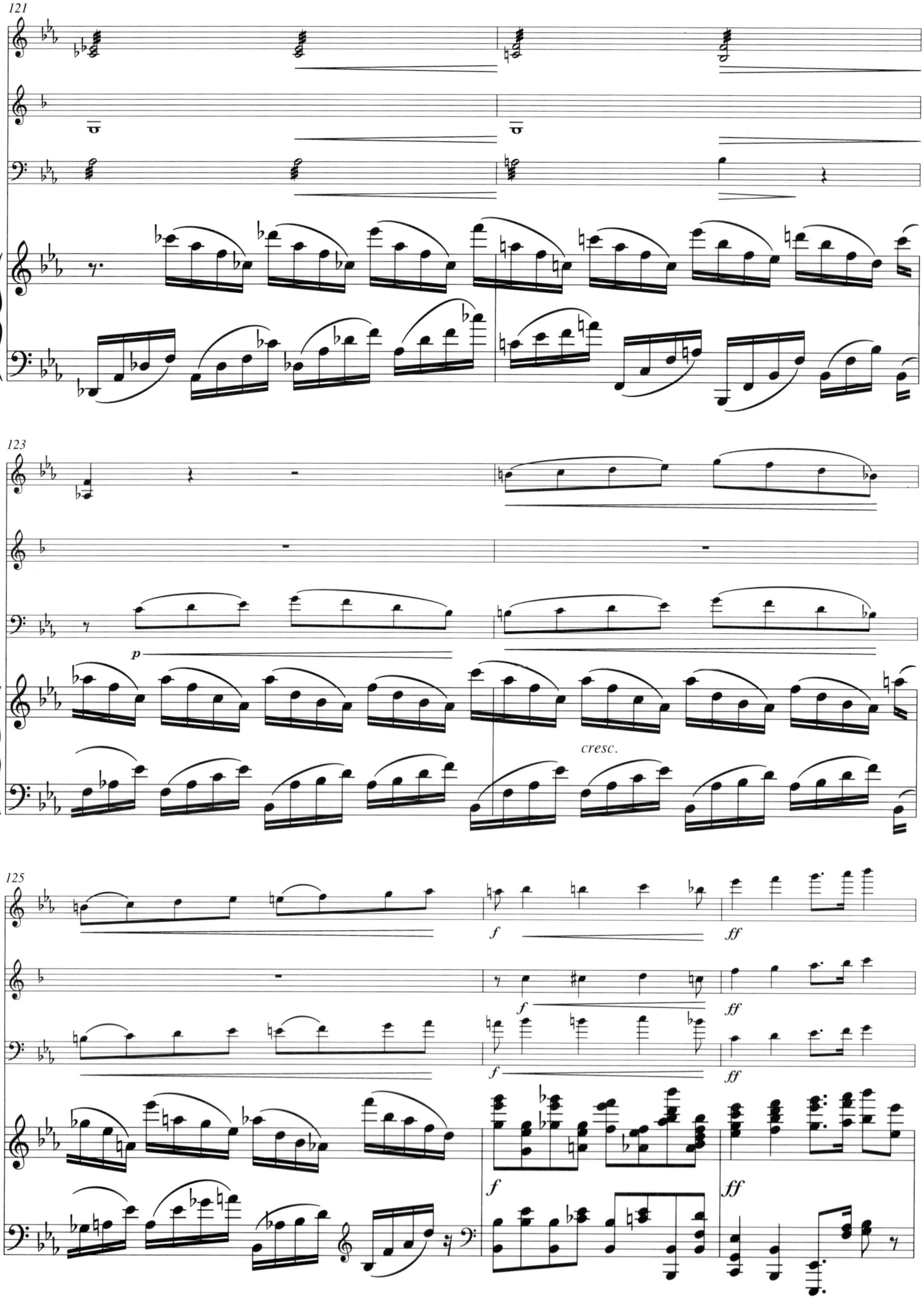
121
123
p
cresc.
125
f
ff

51

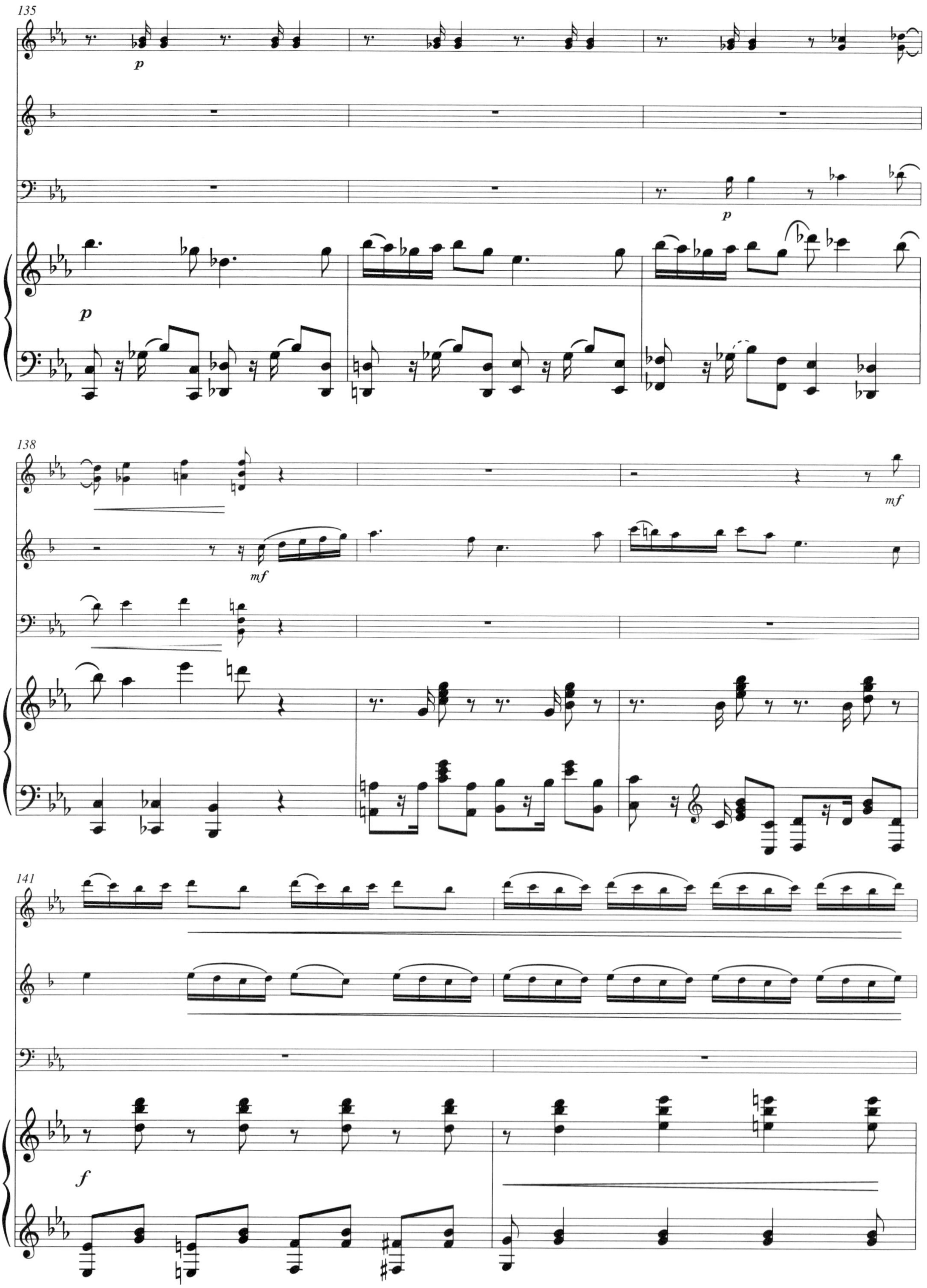
135
p
138
mf
141
f

53

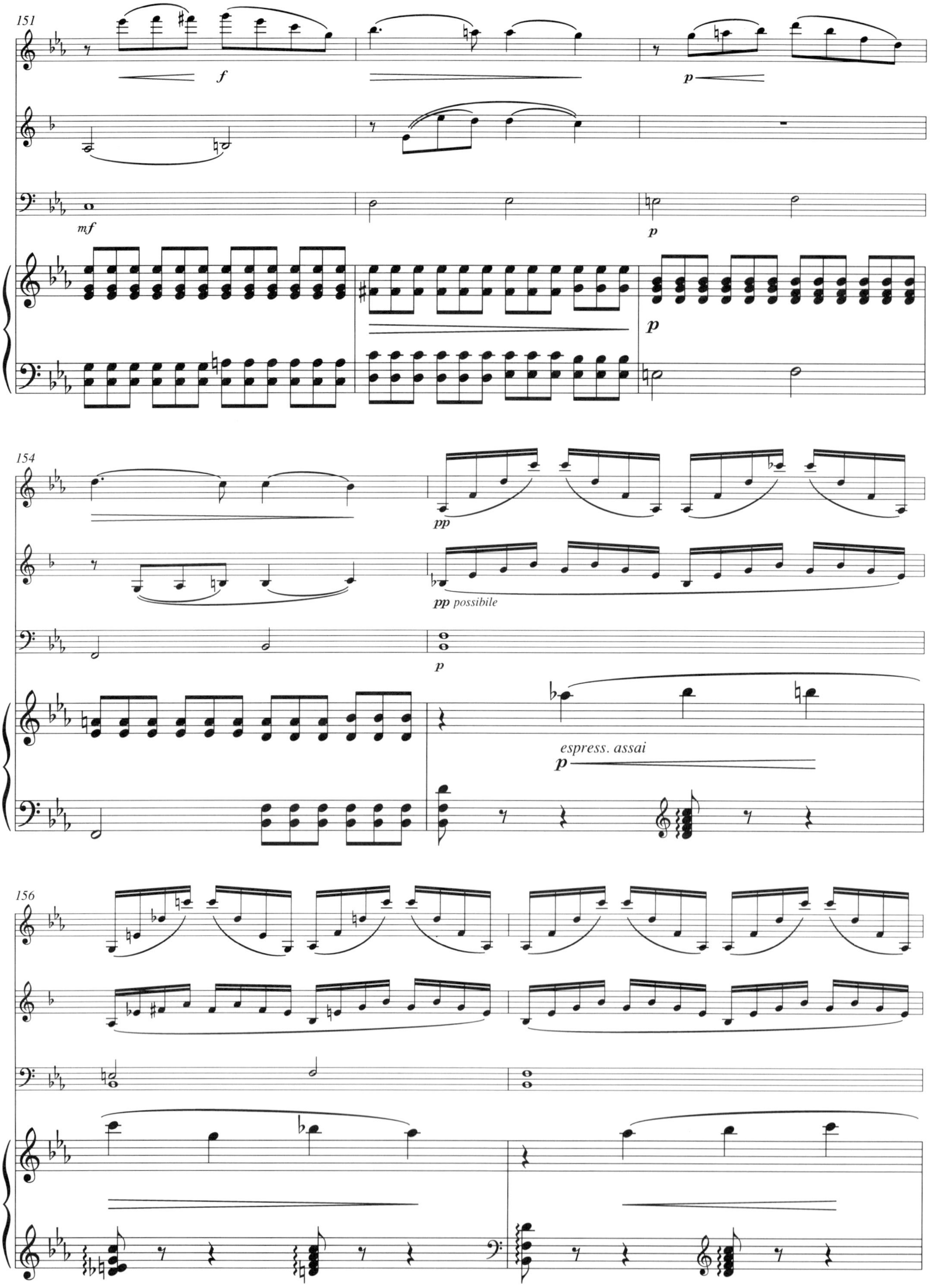
151
f
p
mf
p
p
154
pp
pp possibile
p
espress. assai
p
156

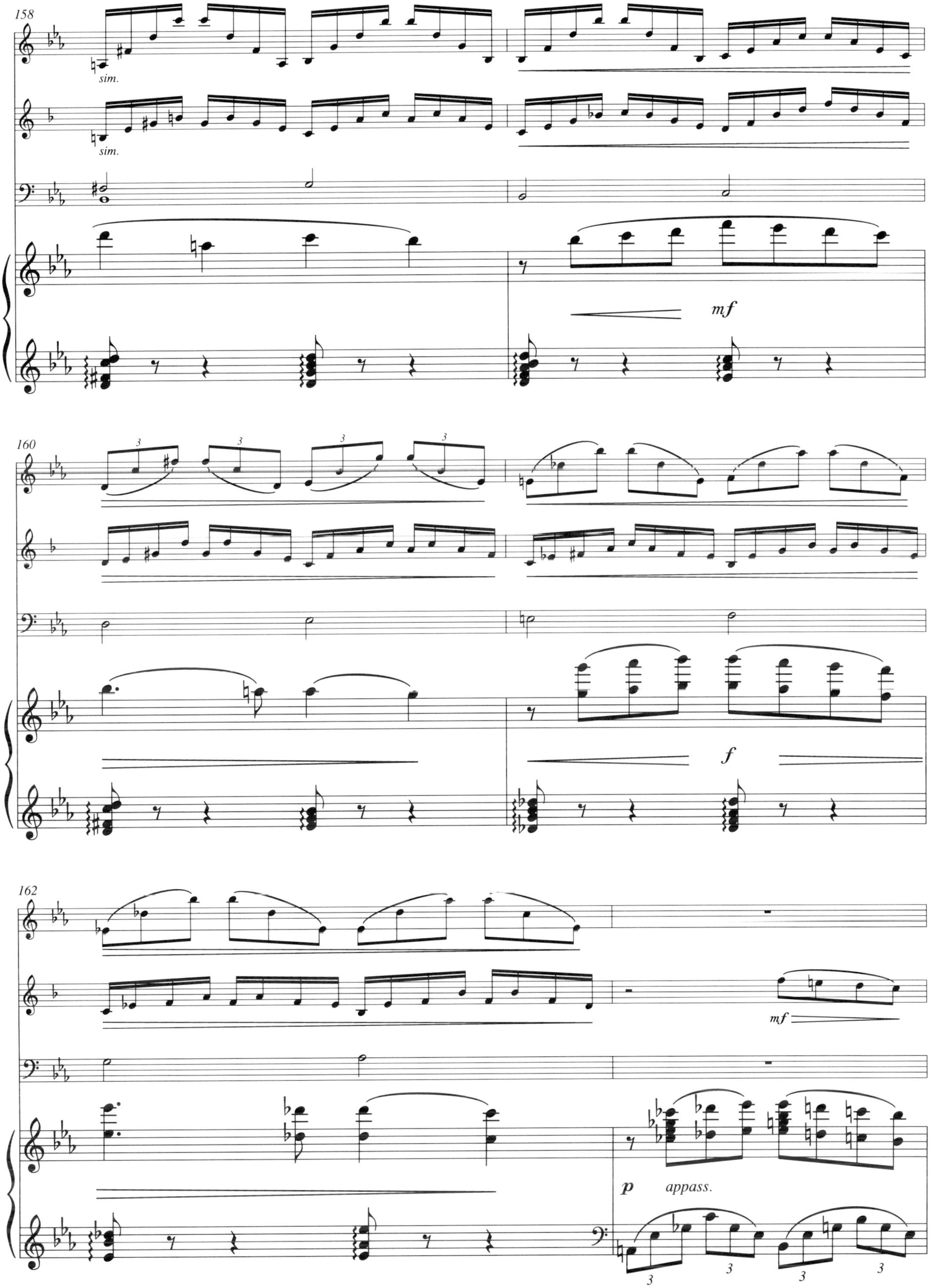
158
sim.
sim.
mf
160
f
162
mf
p
appass.
3

164
8va
167
Presto
p
Presto
(8va)
ff
p
leggiero
p
171
pizz.
arco
p
mf
pizz.

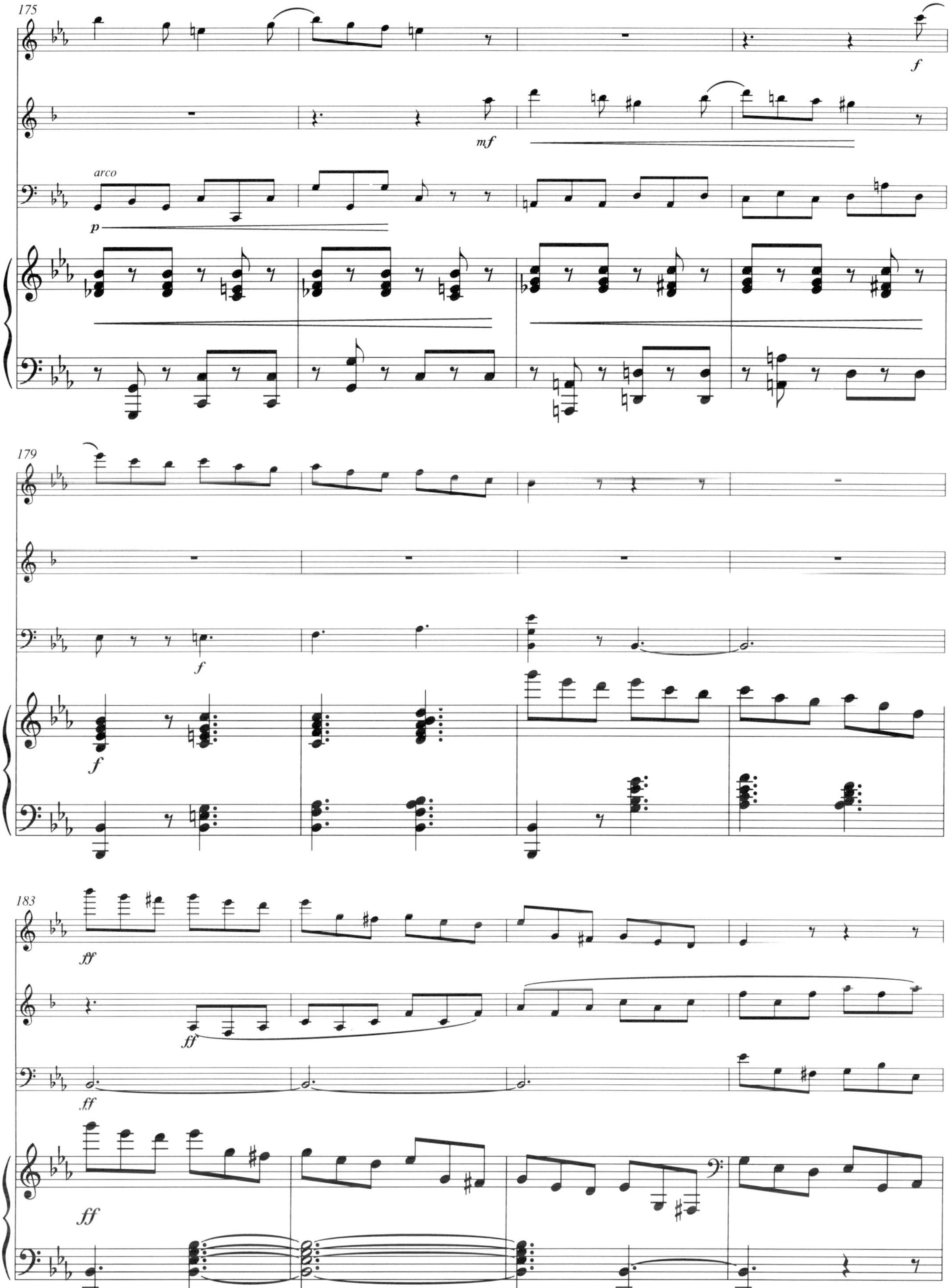
175
arco
p
mf
f
179
f
f
183
ff
ff
ff
ff

187
tr
cresc.
tr
cresc.
ff
tr
4
cresc.
191
Tempo I assai vivace
ff al fine
ff al fine
ff al fine
Tempo I assai vivace
ff al fine
194

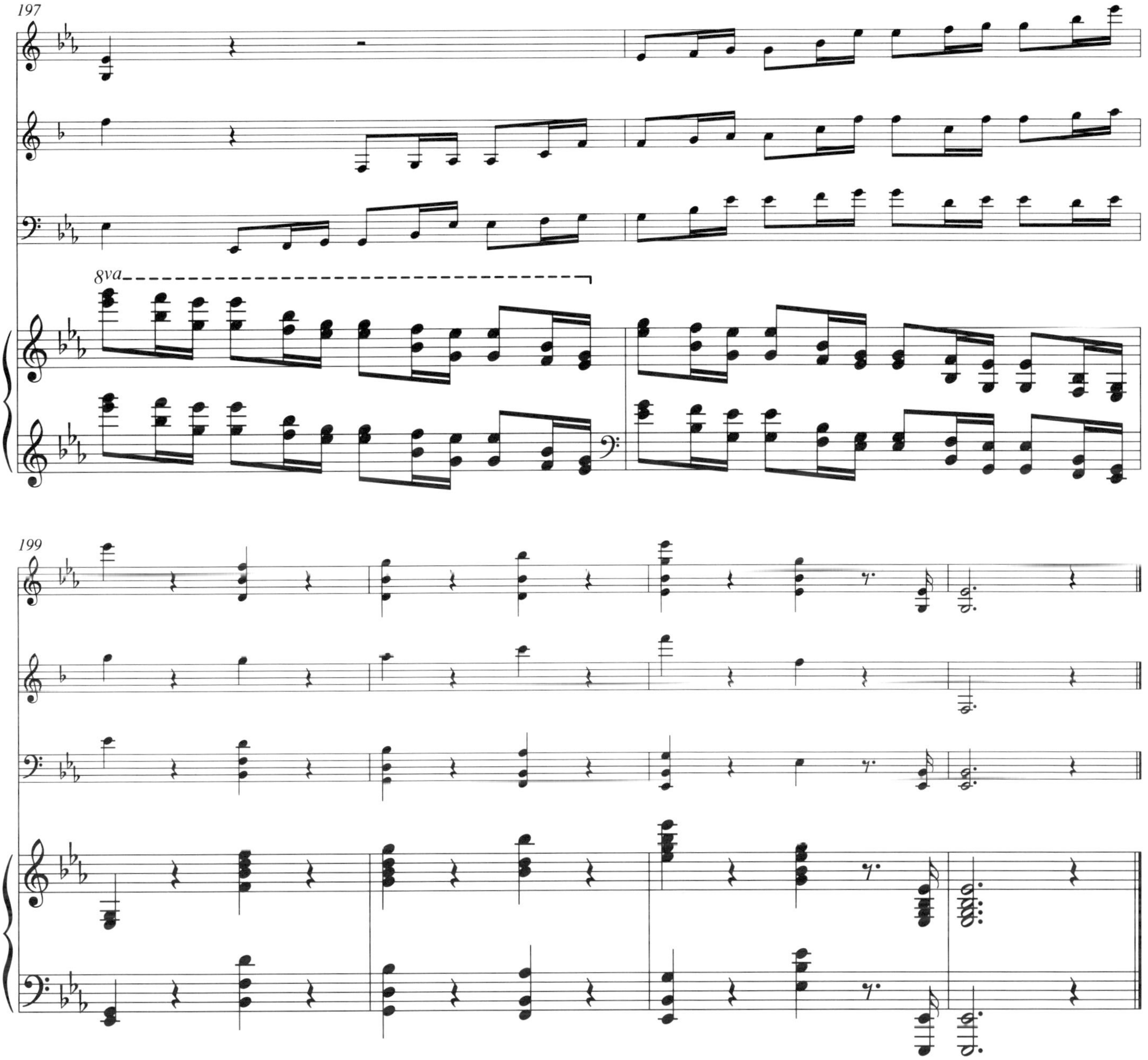
197
8va
199

Fantasiestücke, Op. 2

1

19
dim. e poco rit.
dim. e poco rit.
p
a tempo
p
24
f appass.
3
3
3
3
f appass.
28
p
p
pp
p
p
pp
p
pp

2

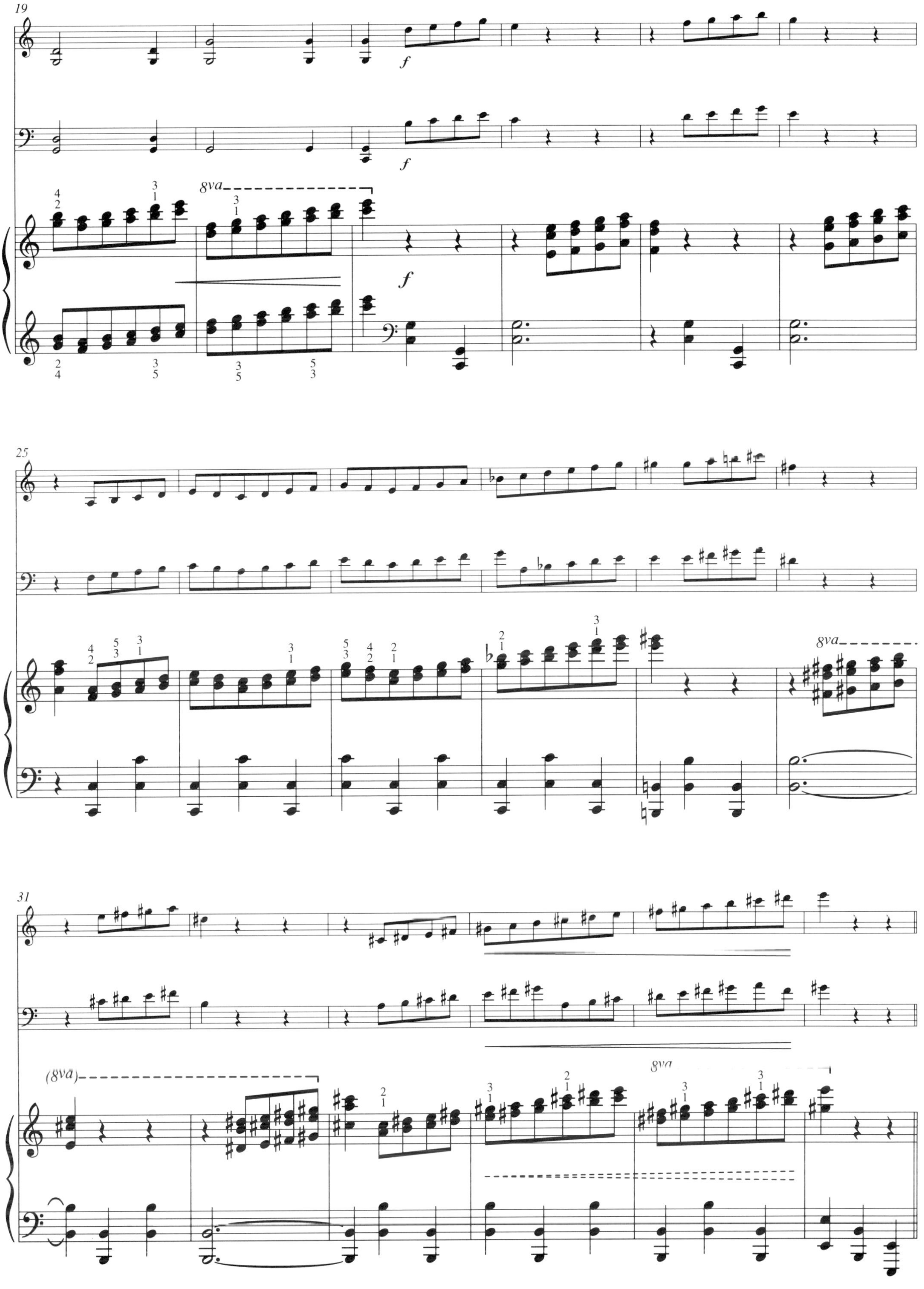
19
f
f
8va
f
25
8va
31
(8va)
8va

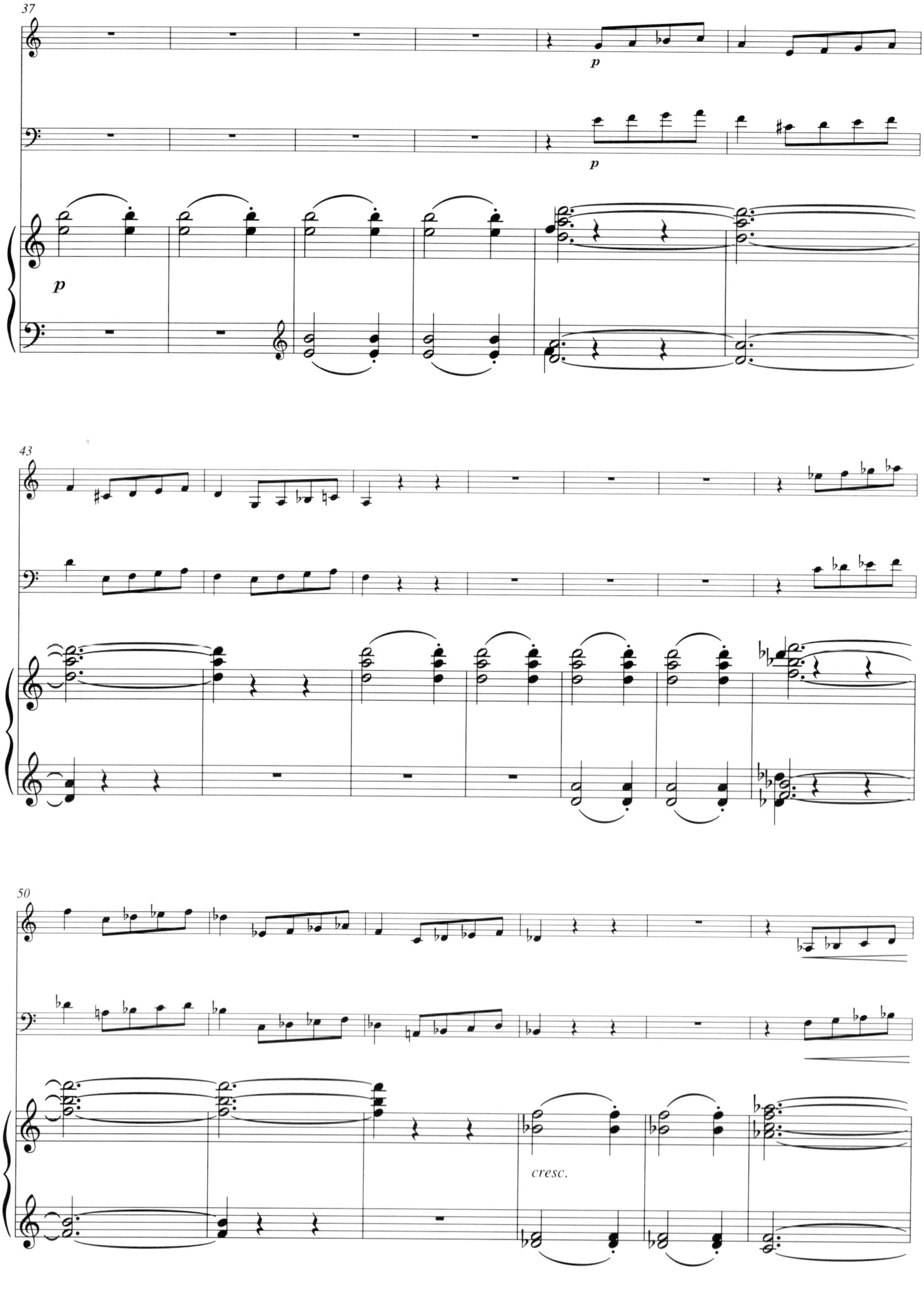
37
p
p
p
43
50
cresc.

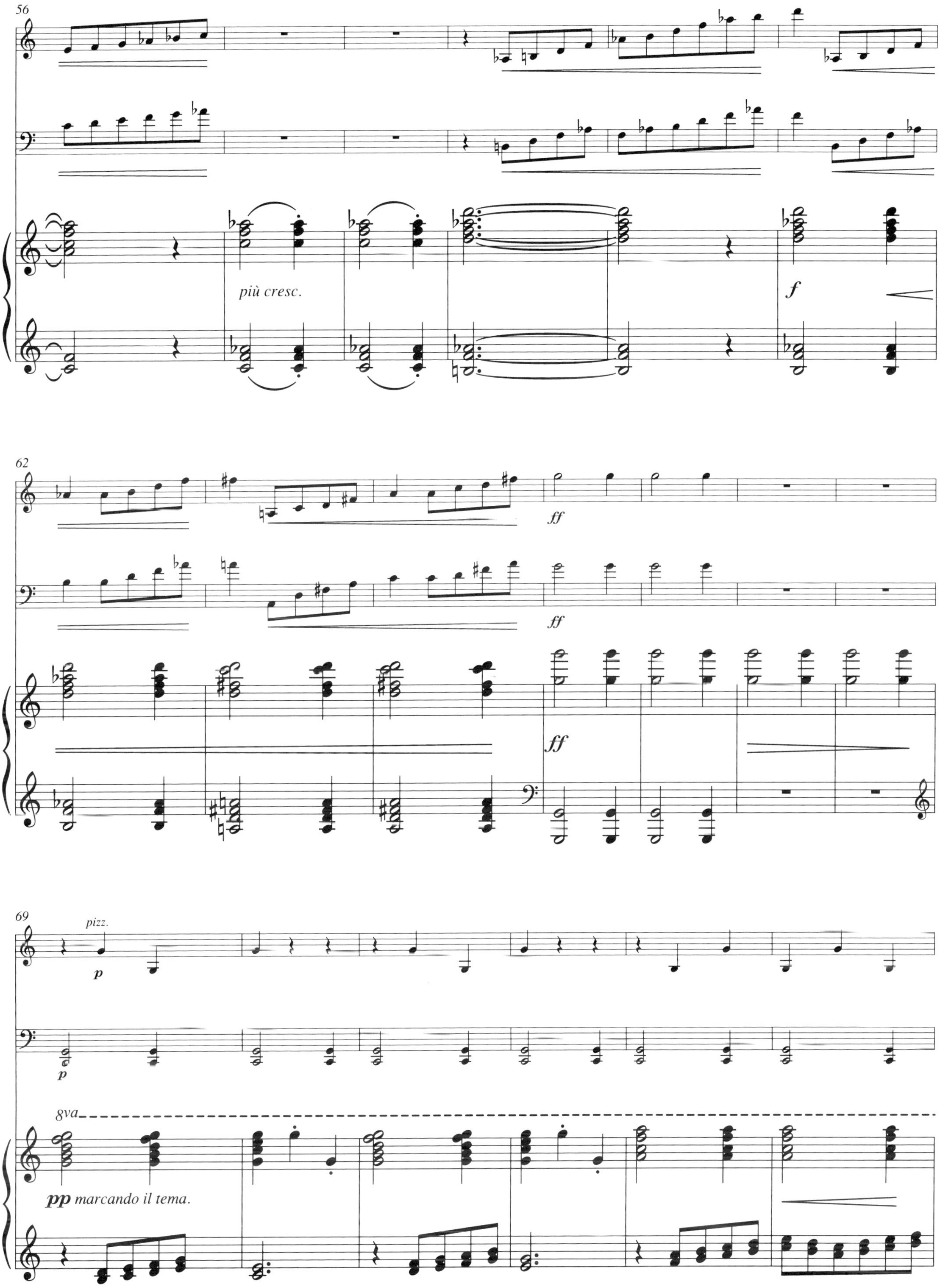
56
più cresc.
f
62
ff
ff
ff
69
pizz.
p
p
8va
pp marcando il tema.

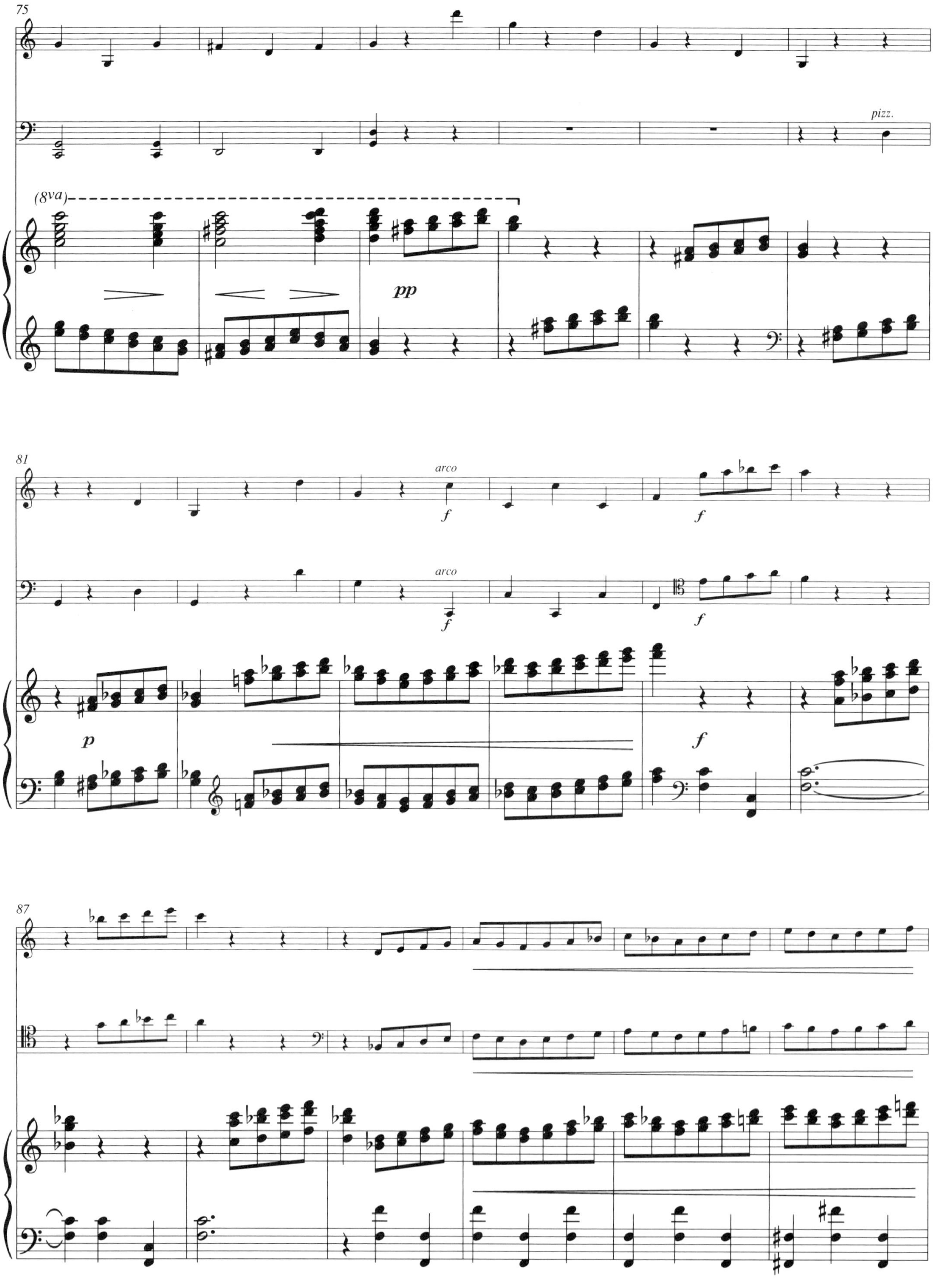
75
pizz.
(8va)
pp
81
arco
arco
f
f
f
f
p
f
87

67

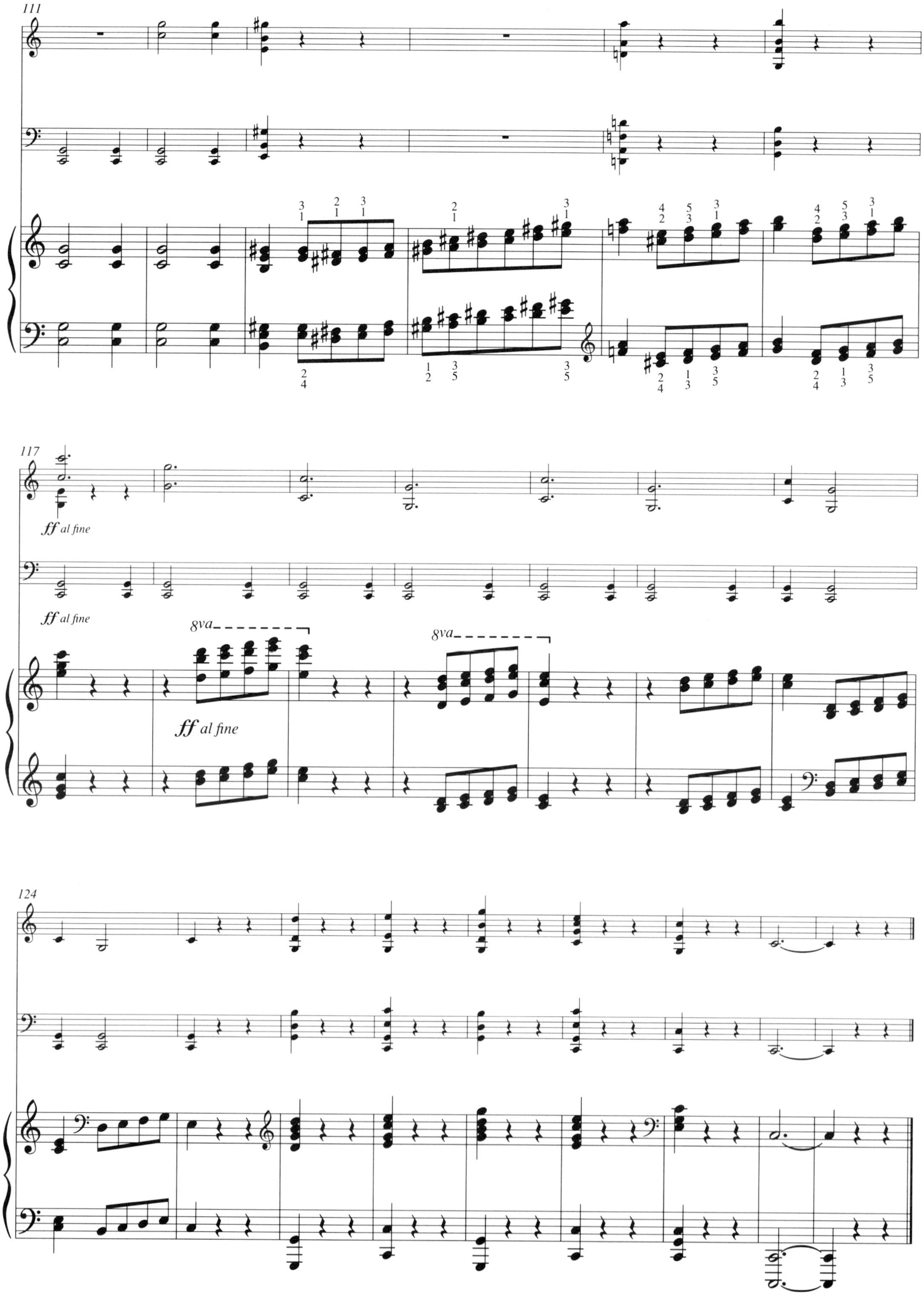
111
117
ff al fine
ff al fine
8va
ff al fine
8va
124

3

9
pizz.
p
pizz.
p
p
12
pp
rit.
pp
rit.
pp
p rit.
15
a tempo
cresc.
arco
ff
a tempo
cresc.
arco
ff
a tempo
cresc.
ff

4

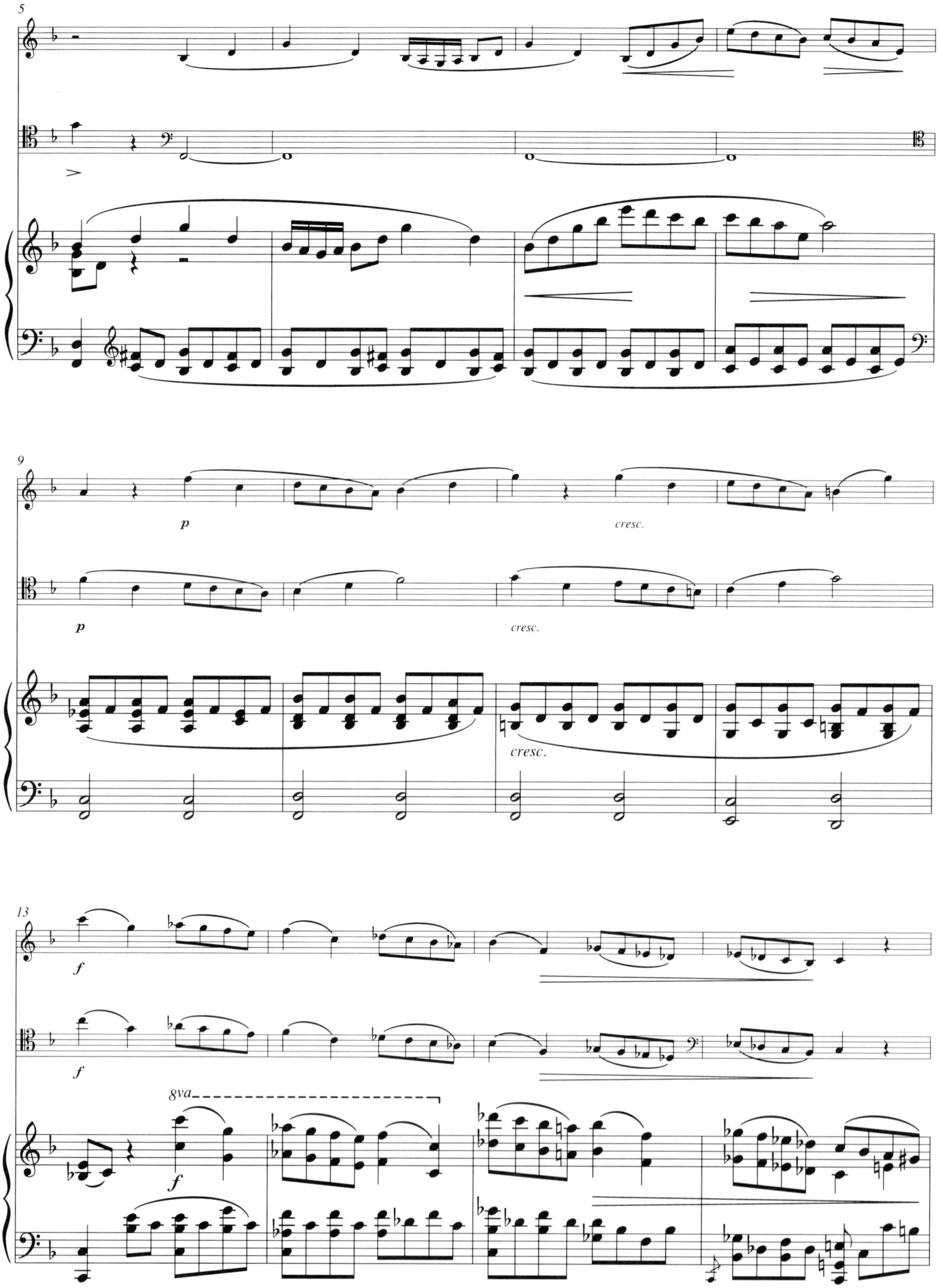
5
9
p
p
cresc.
cresc.
cresc.
13
f
f
8va
f

17
pp
pp
pp e legatissimo
espress.
21
p
mf
p
mf
p
24
f
pp dolcissimo
f
pp dolcissimo
f
pp dolcissimo

5

75

76

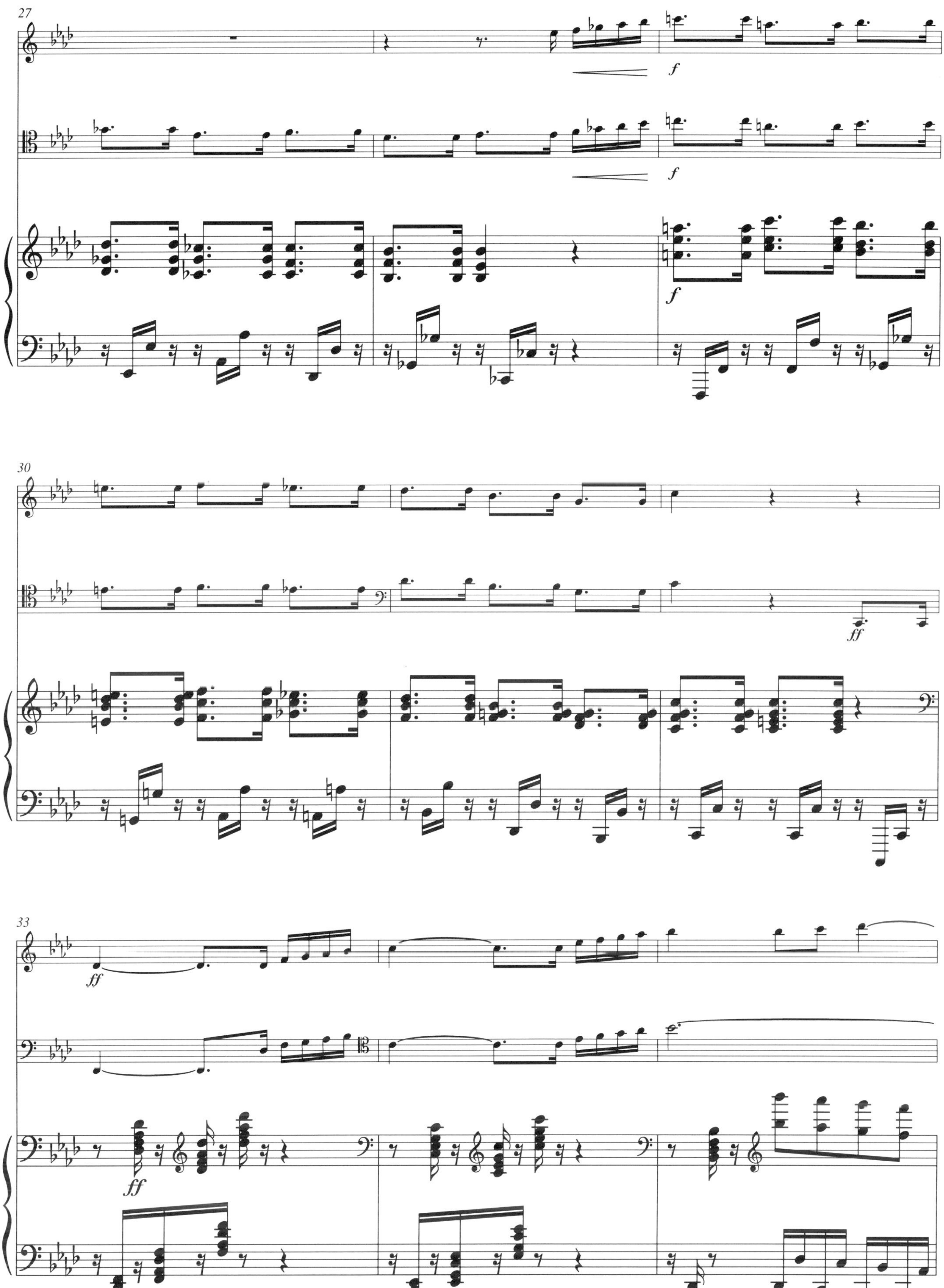
27
f
f
f
30
ff
33
ff
ff

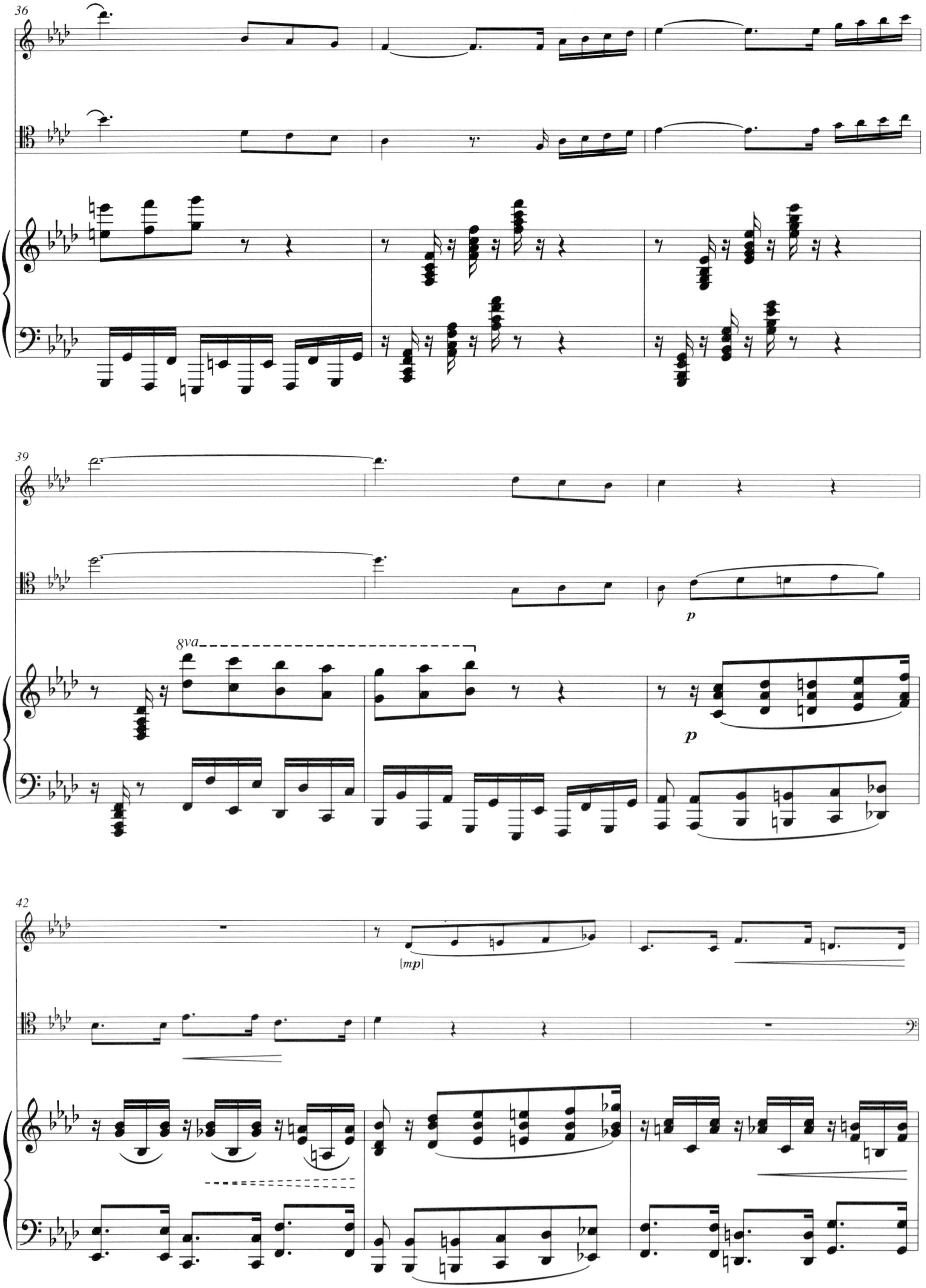
36
39
8va
p
p
42
[mp]

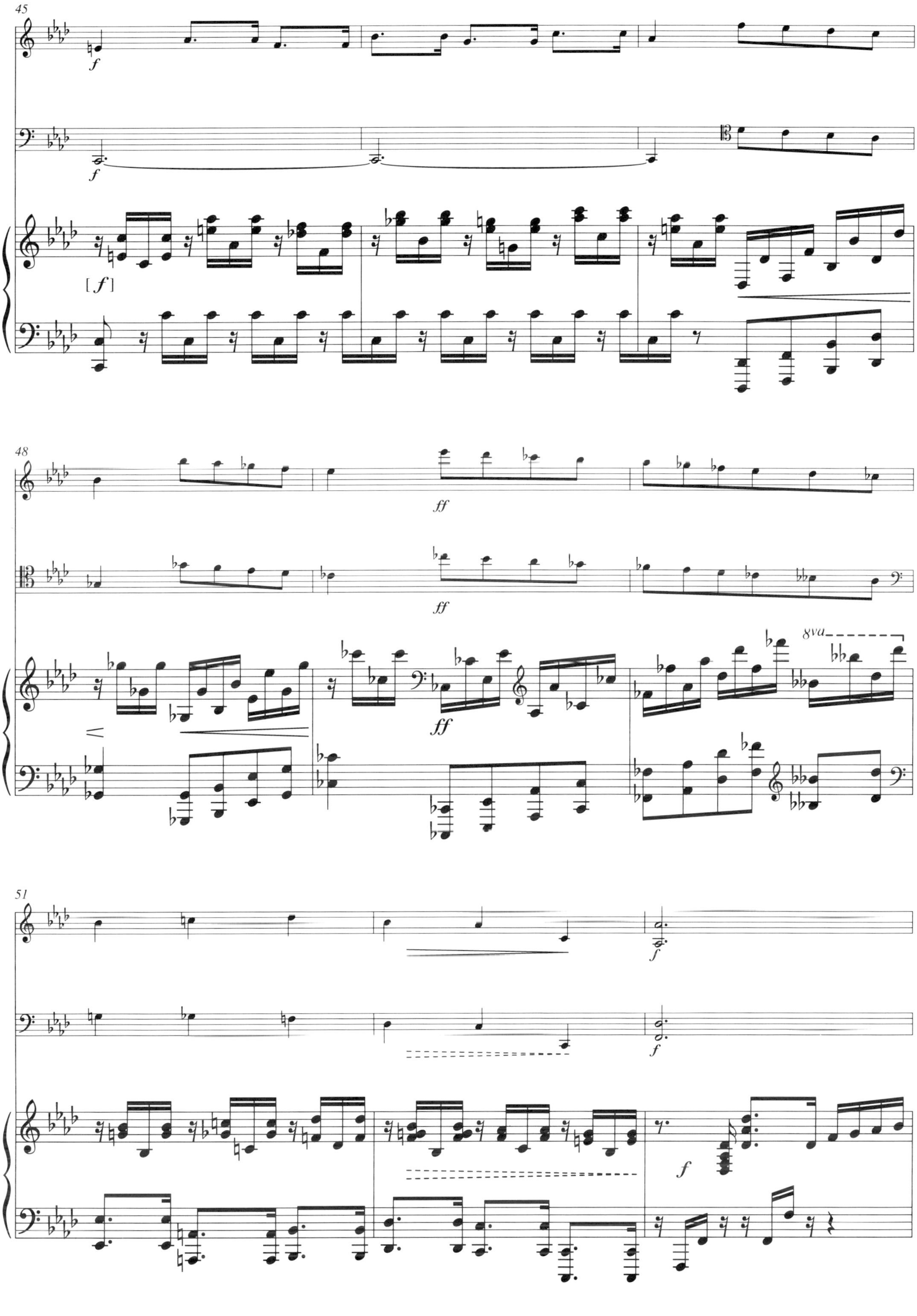
45
48
51
8va

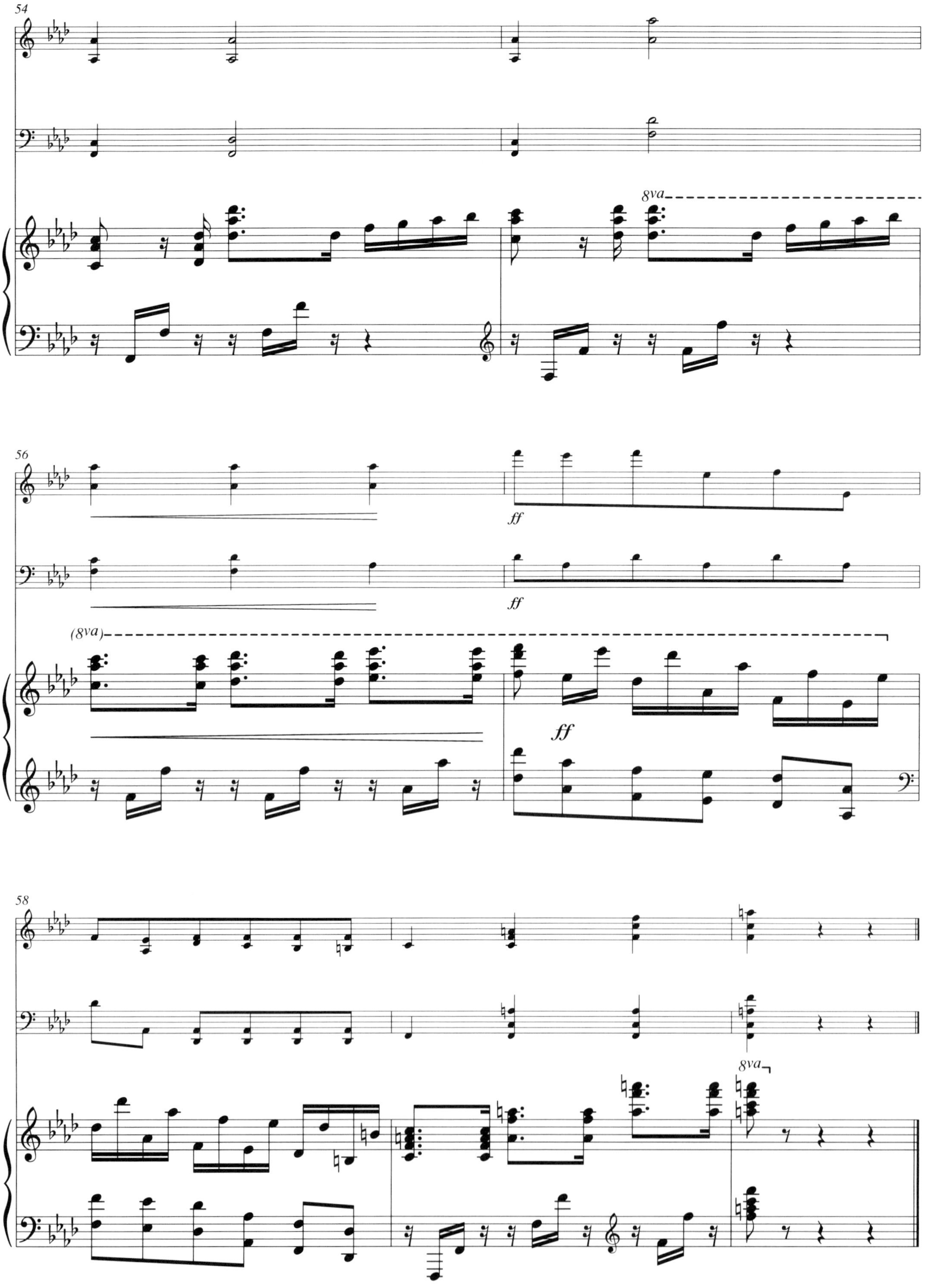

54
8va
56
ff
ff
(8va)
ff
58
8va

6

16
p
p
mf
21
1.
2.
10
p
pp
26
Poco meno mosso
p
espress.
ff
mf
Poco meno mosso
mf
p
rit. un poco
p tre corde

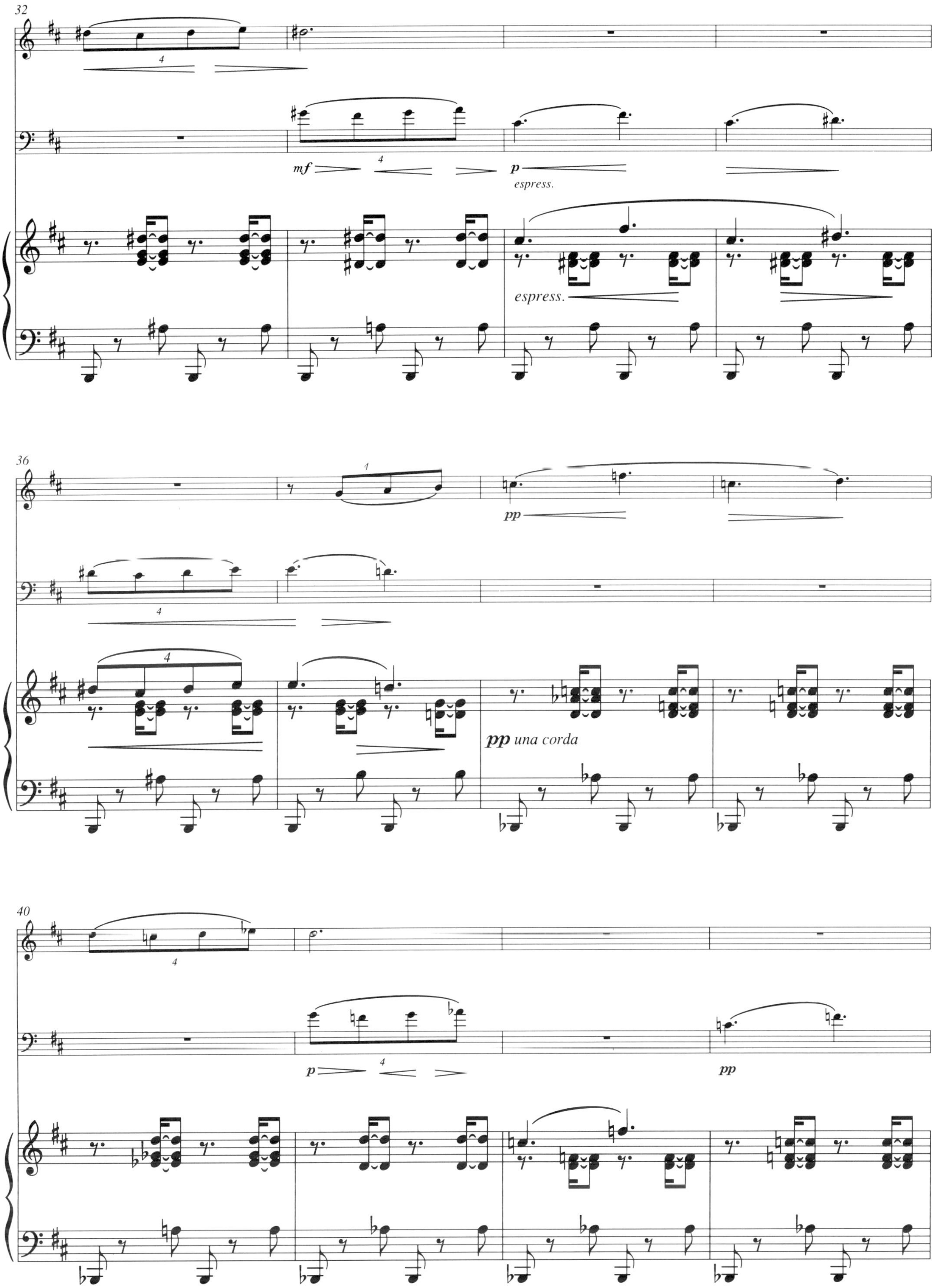
32
mf
p
espress.
espress.
36
pp
pp una corda
40
p
pp

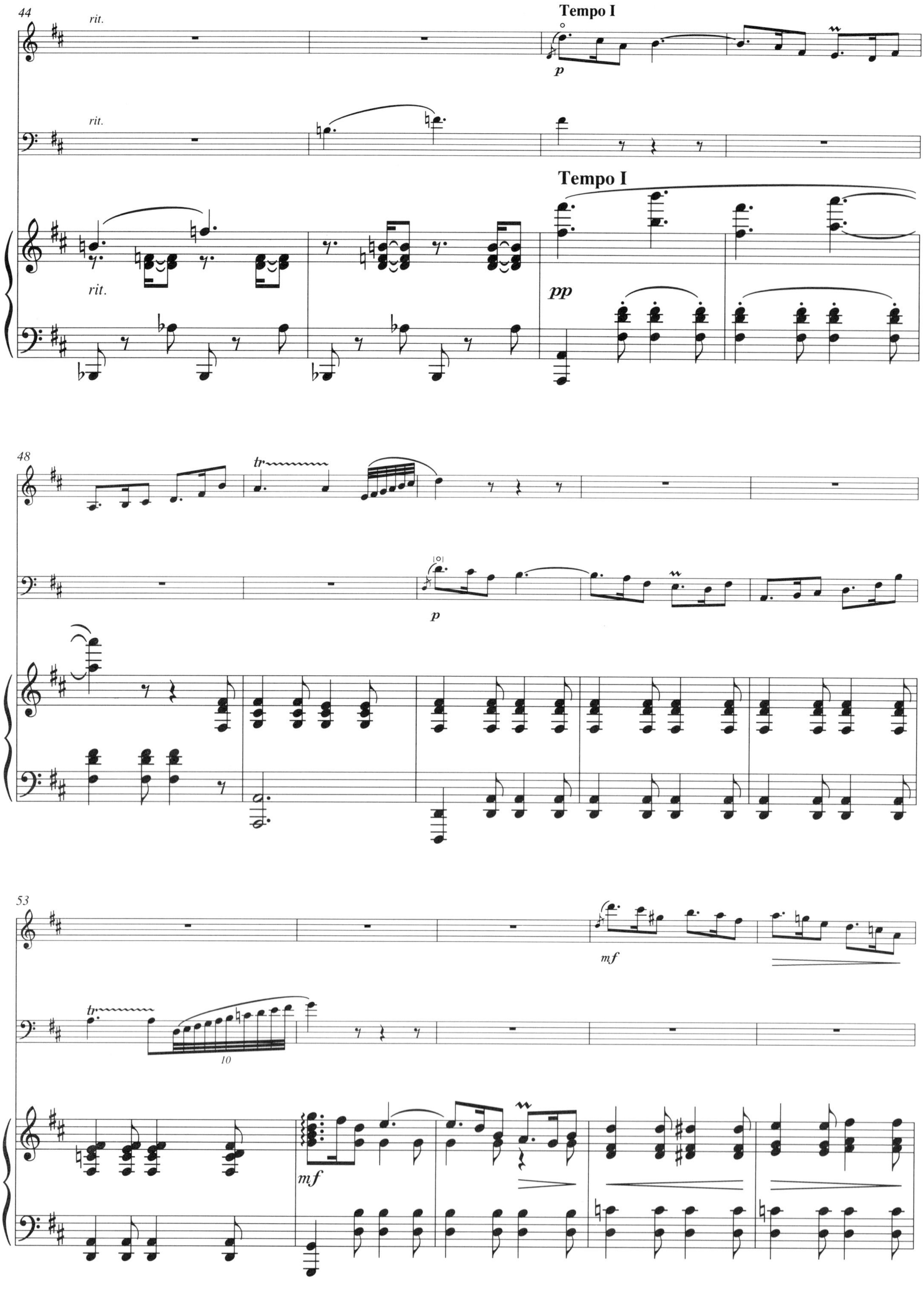
44
rit.
Tempo I
p
rit.
Tempo I
rit.
pp
48
tr
p
53
tr
10
mf
mf

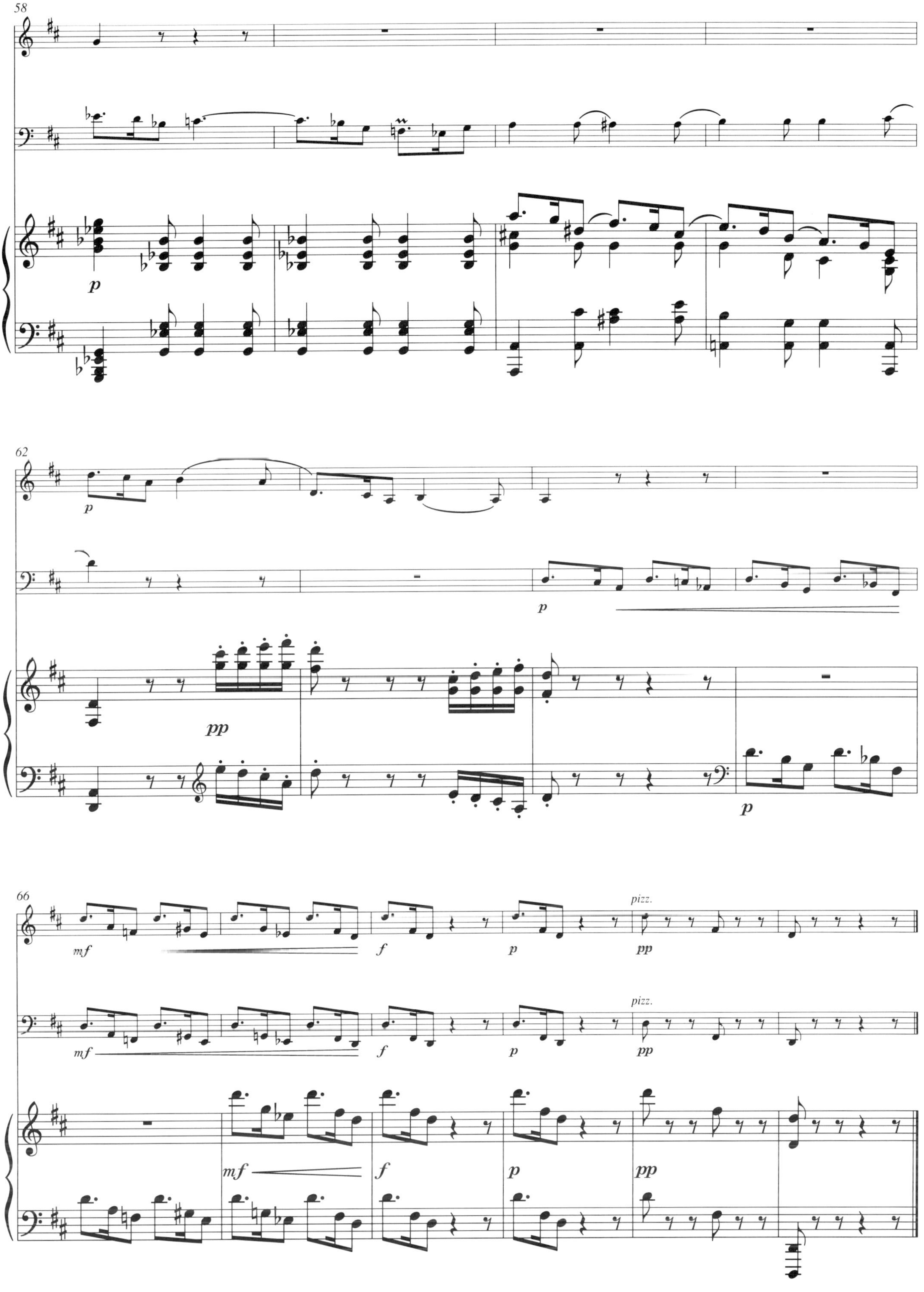
58
p
62
p
pp
p
p
66
mf
f
p
pizz.
pp
mf
f
p
pizz.
pp
mf
f
p
pp

7

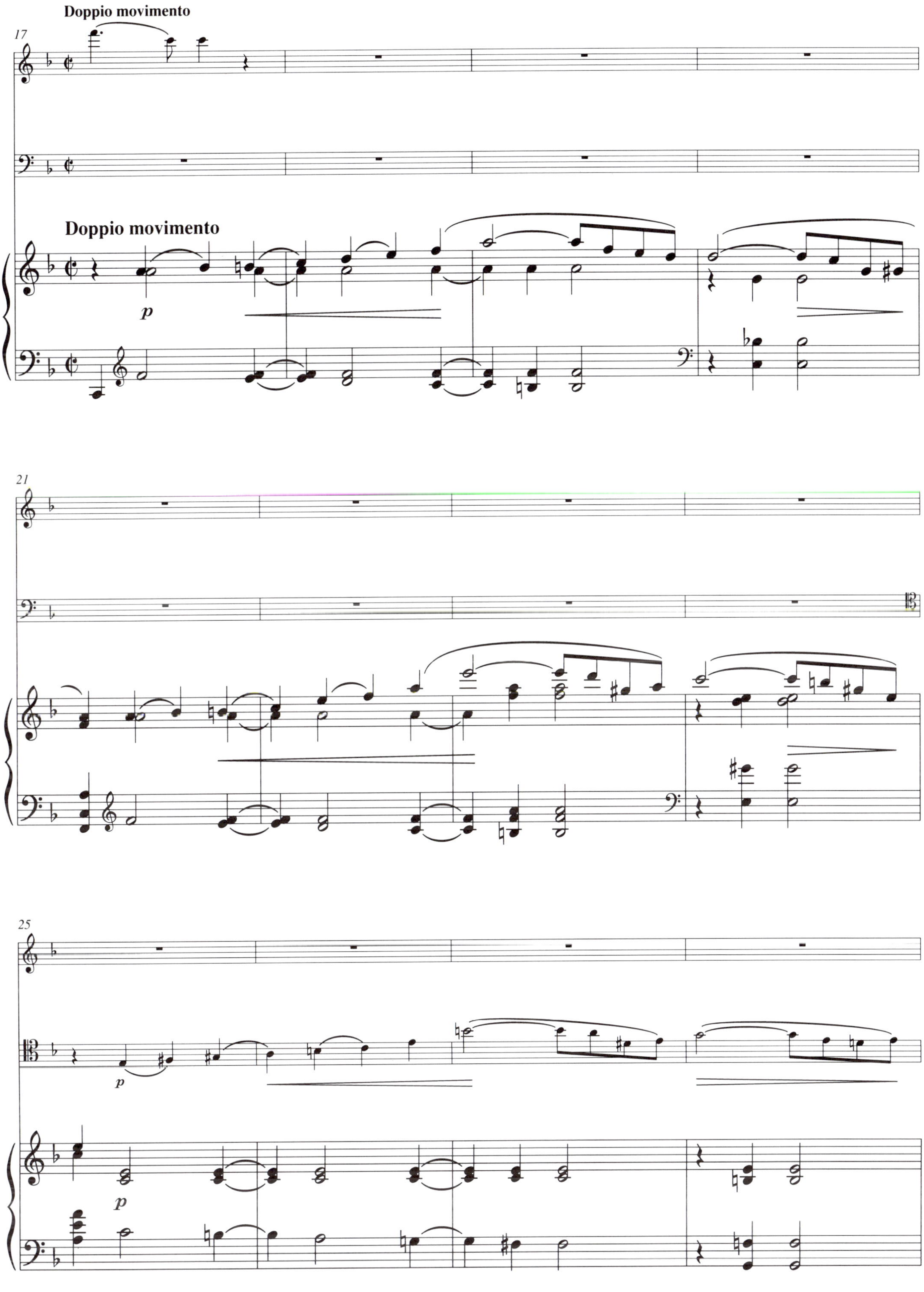
Doppio movimento
17
Doppio movimento
p
21
25
p
p

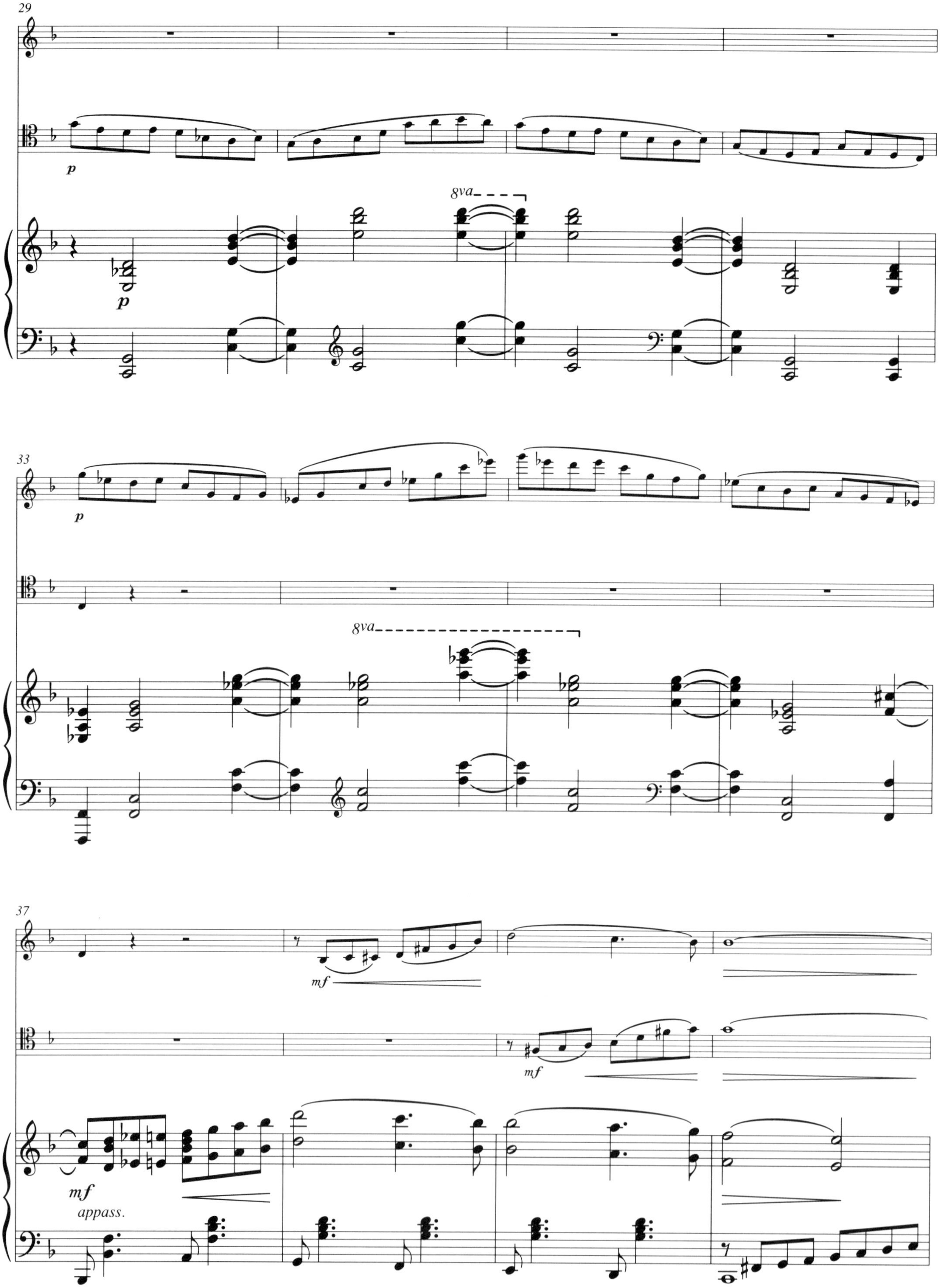
8va
p
appass.
mf

89

51
rit.
al
(8va)
3
6
rit.
al
53
Largo come sopra
ff
p
p espress.
Largo come sopra
ff
p
58
espress.
attacca
rit.
attacca
pp
rit.
attacca
coll 8va

8

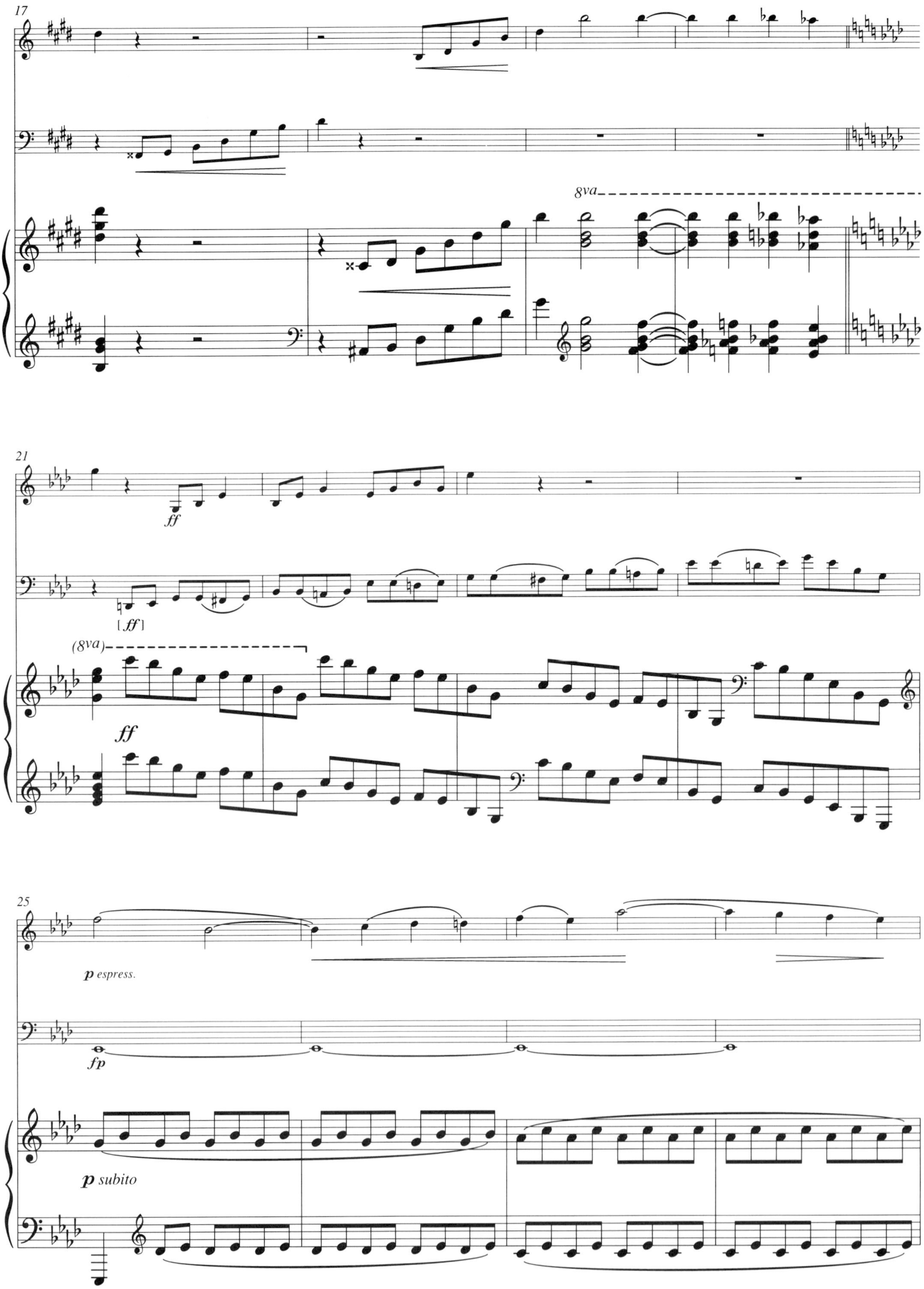
17
8va
21
ff
[ff]
(8va)
ff
25
p espress.
fp
p subito

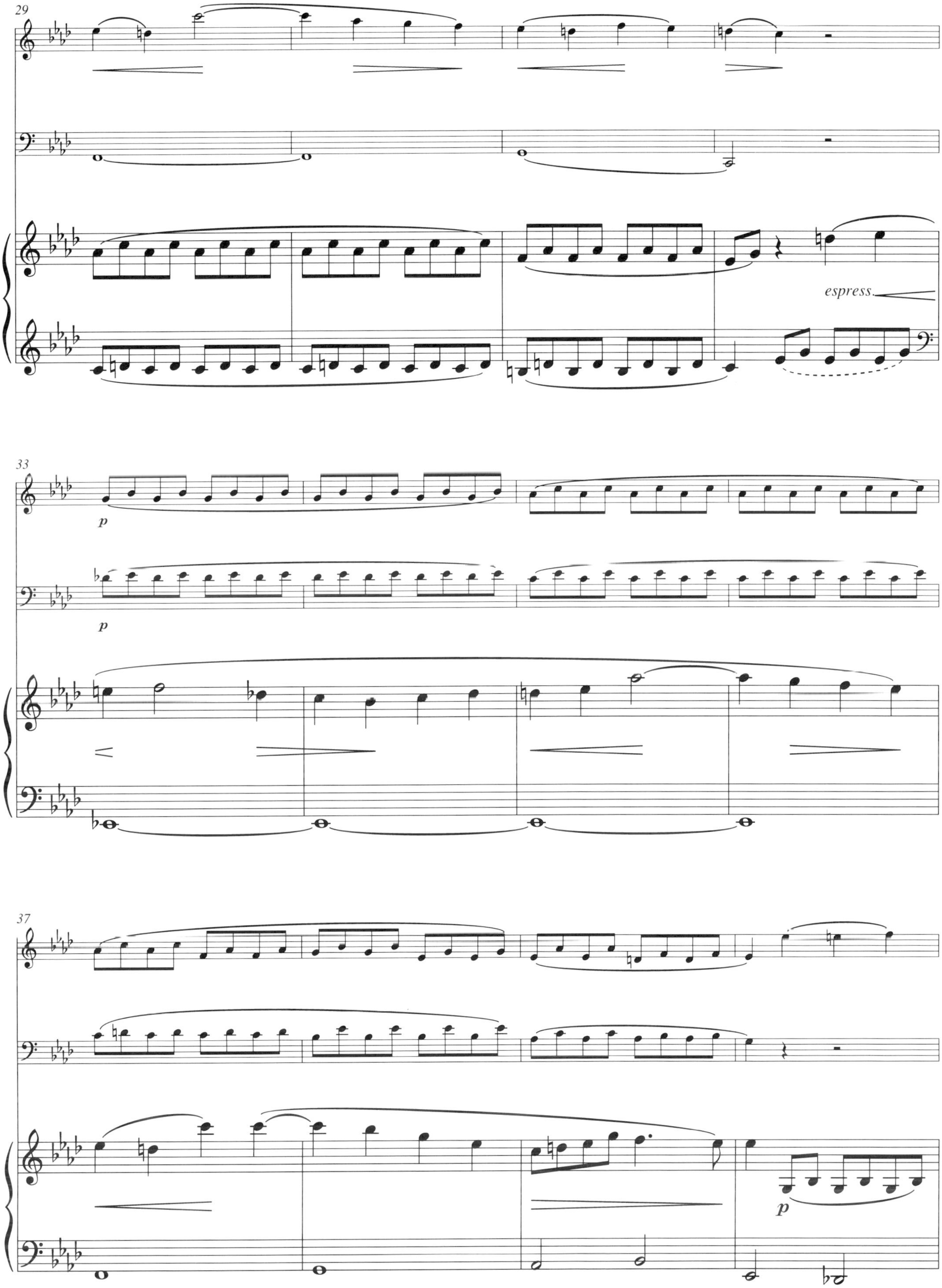
29
espress.
33
p
p
37
p

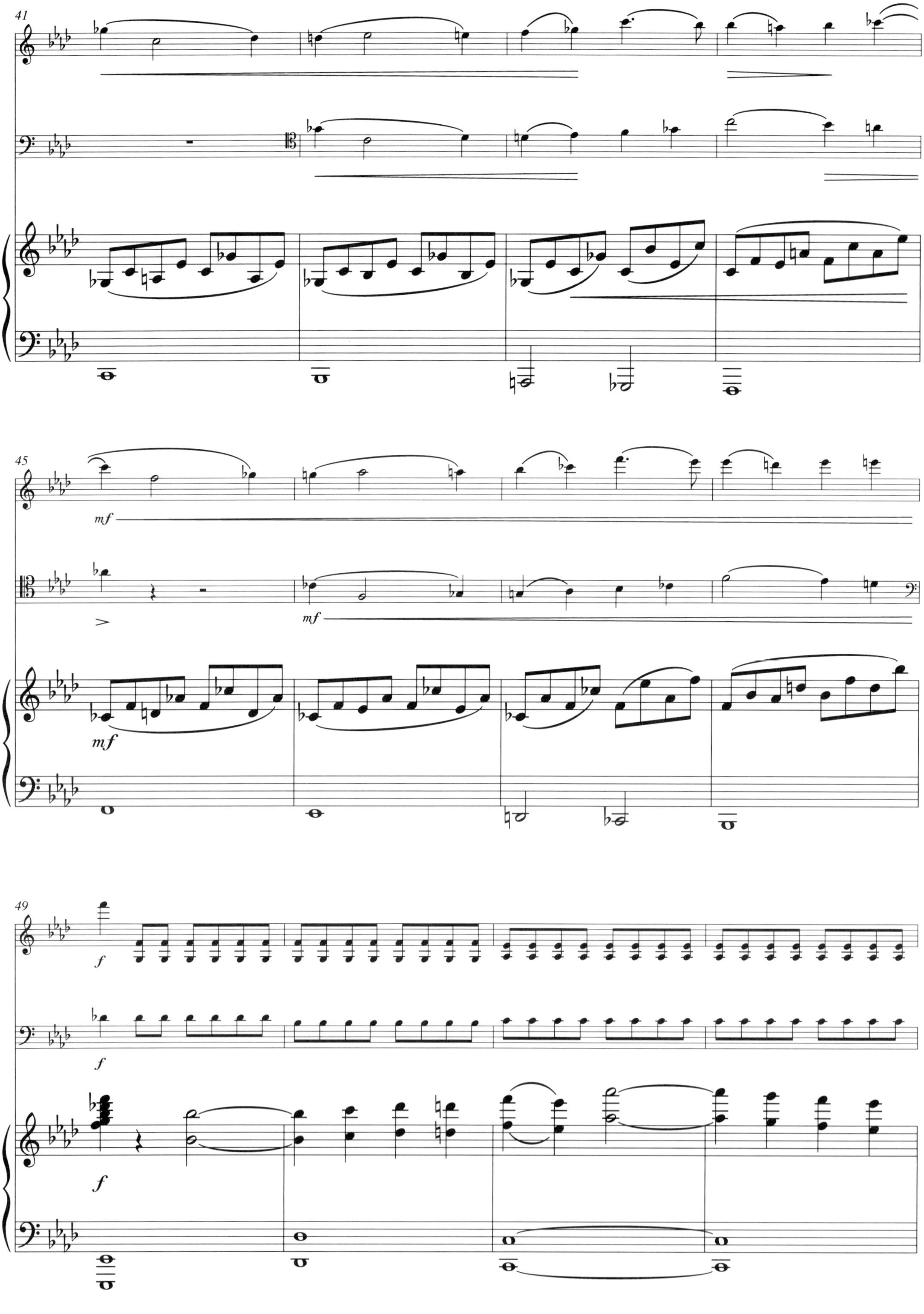
41
mf
45
mf
mf
49
f
f
f

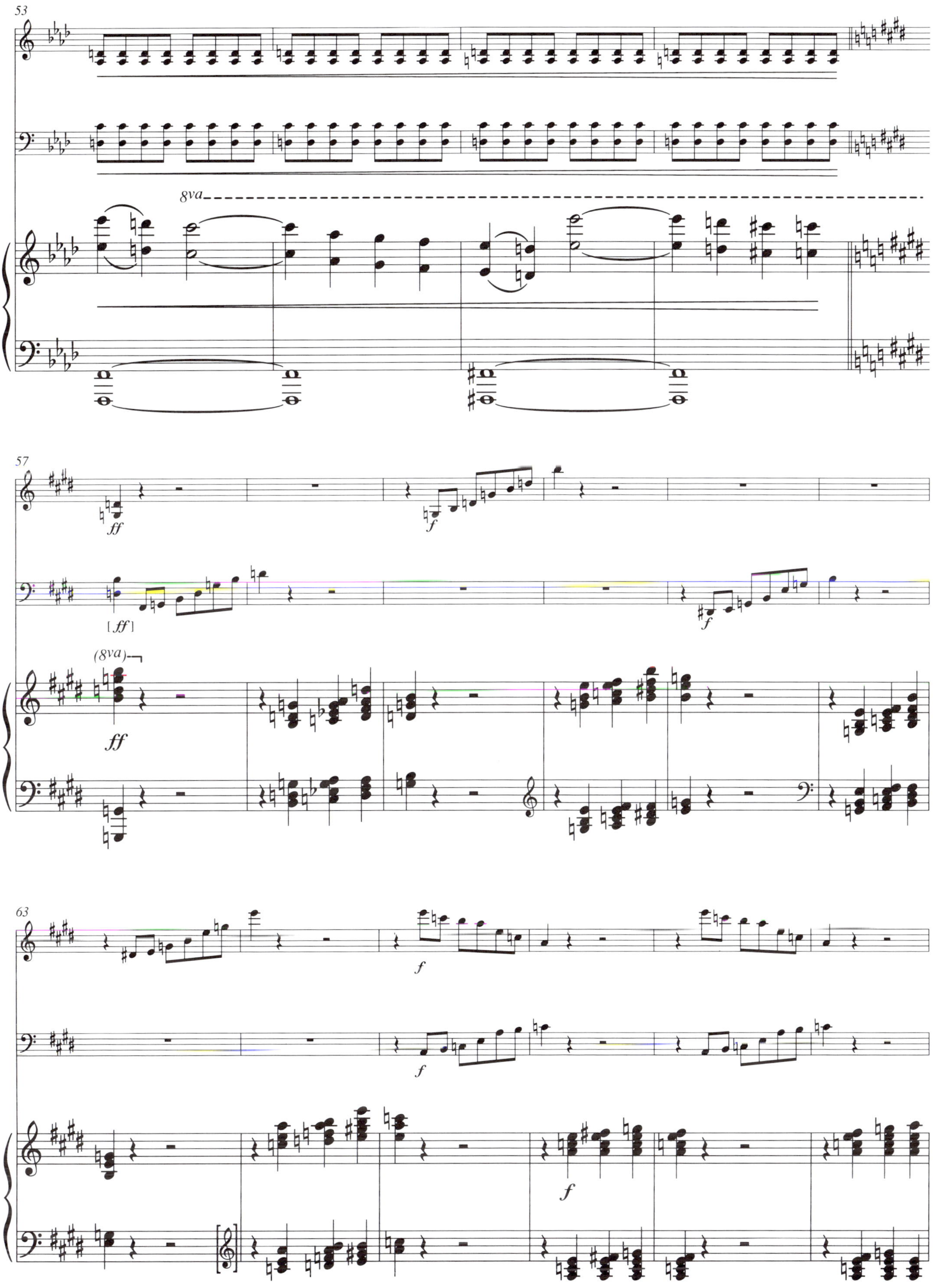
53
8va
57
ff
[ff]
(8va)
ff
f
f
63
f
f
f

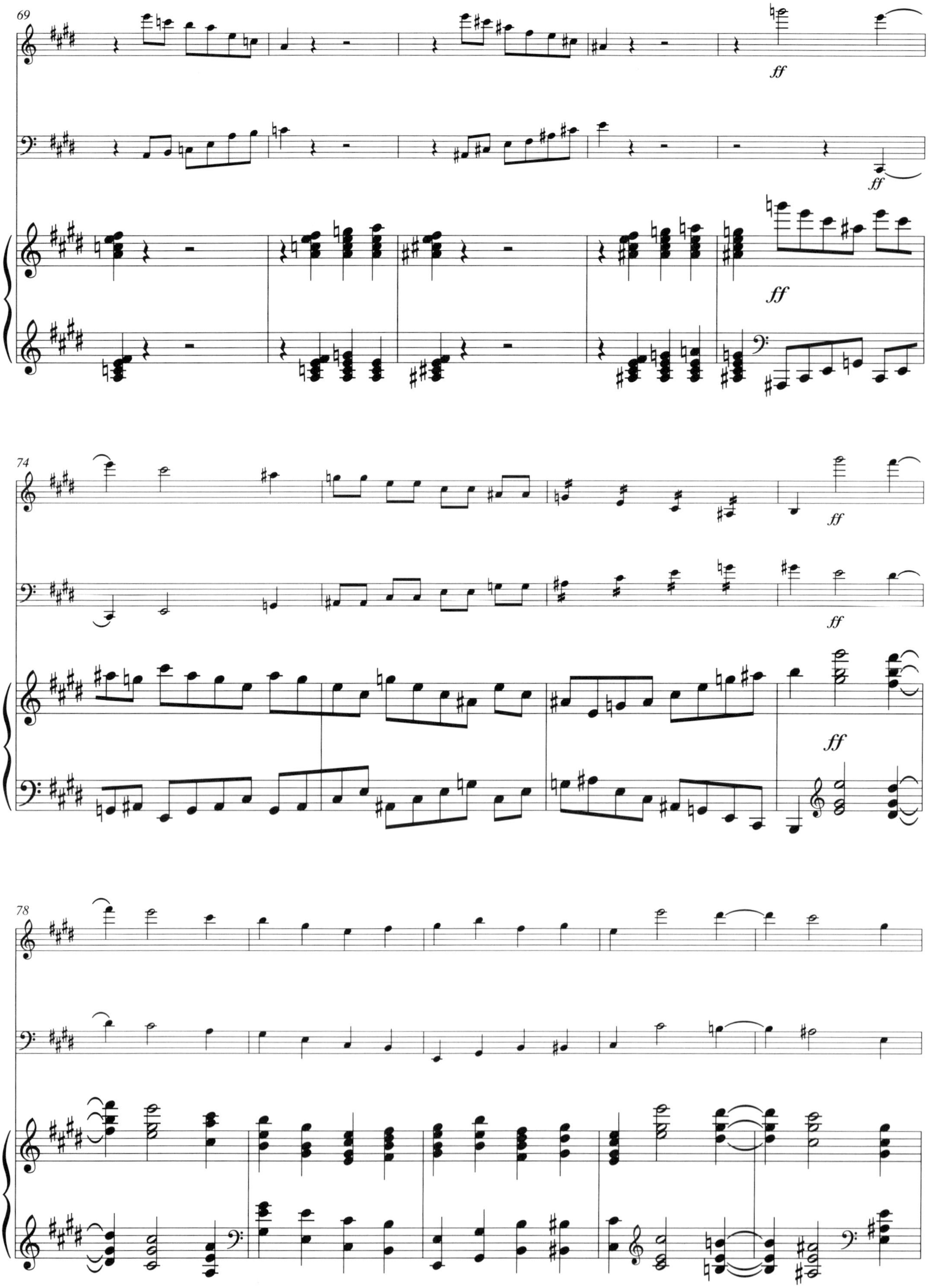
69
ff
ff
ff
74
ff
ff
ff
78

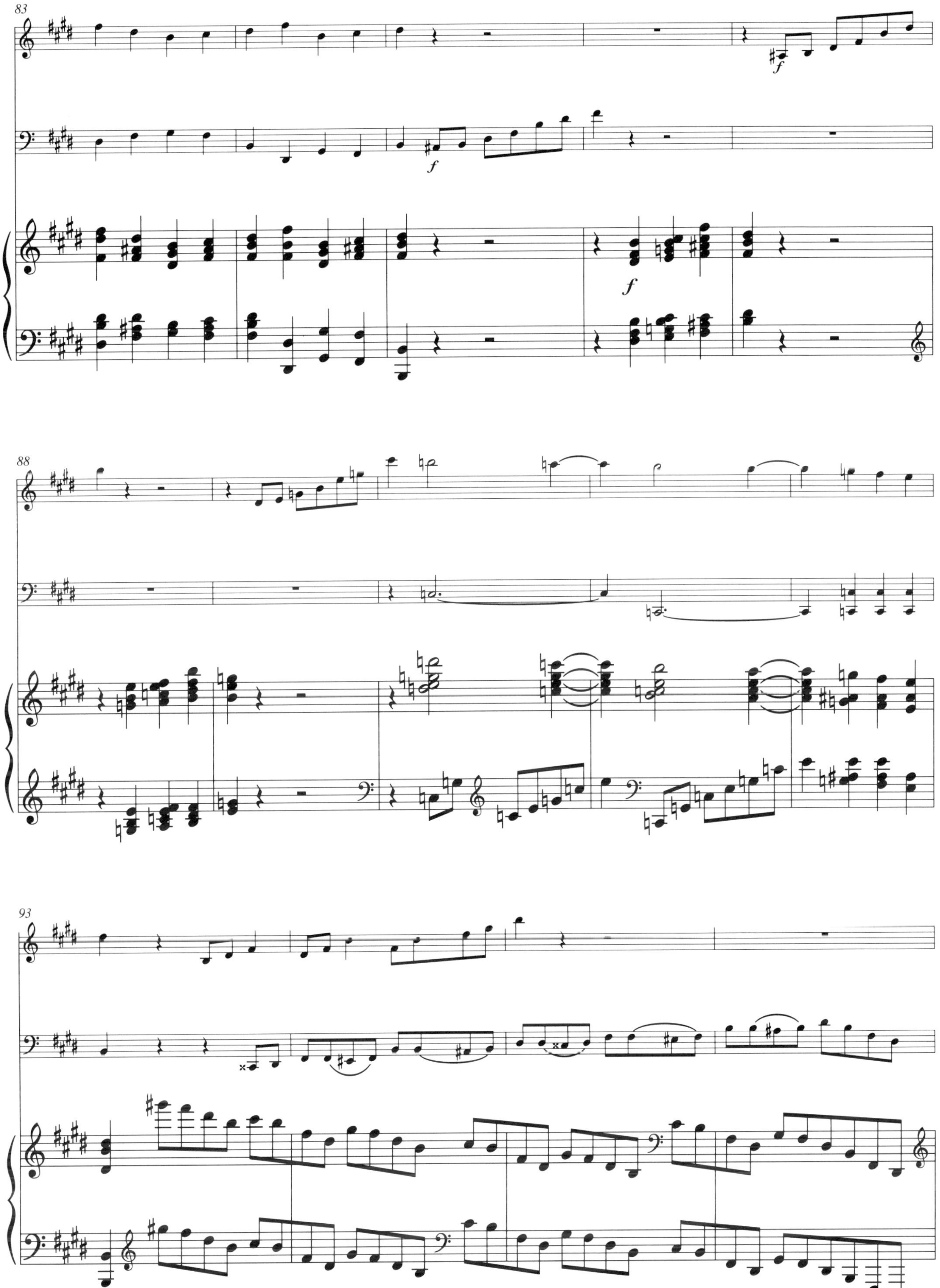
83
f
f
f
88
93

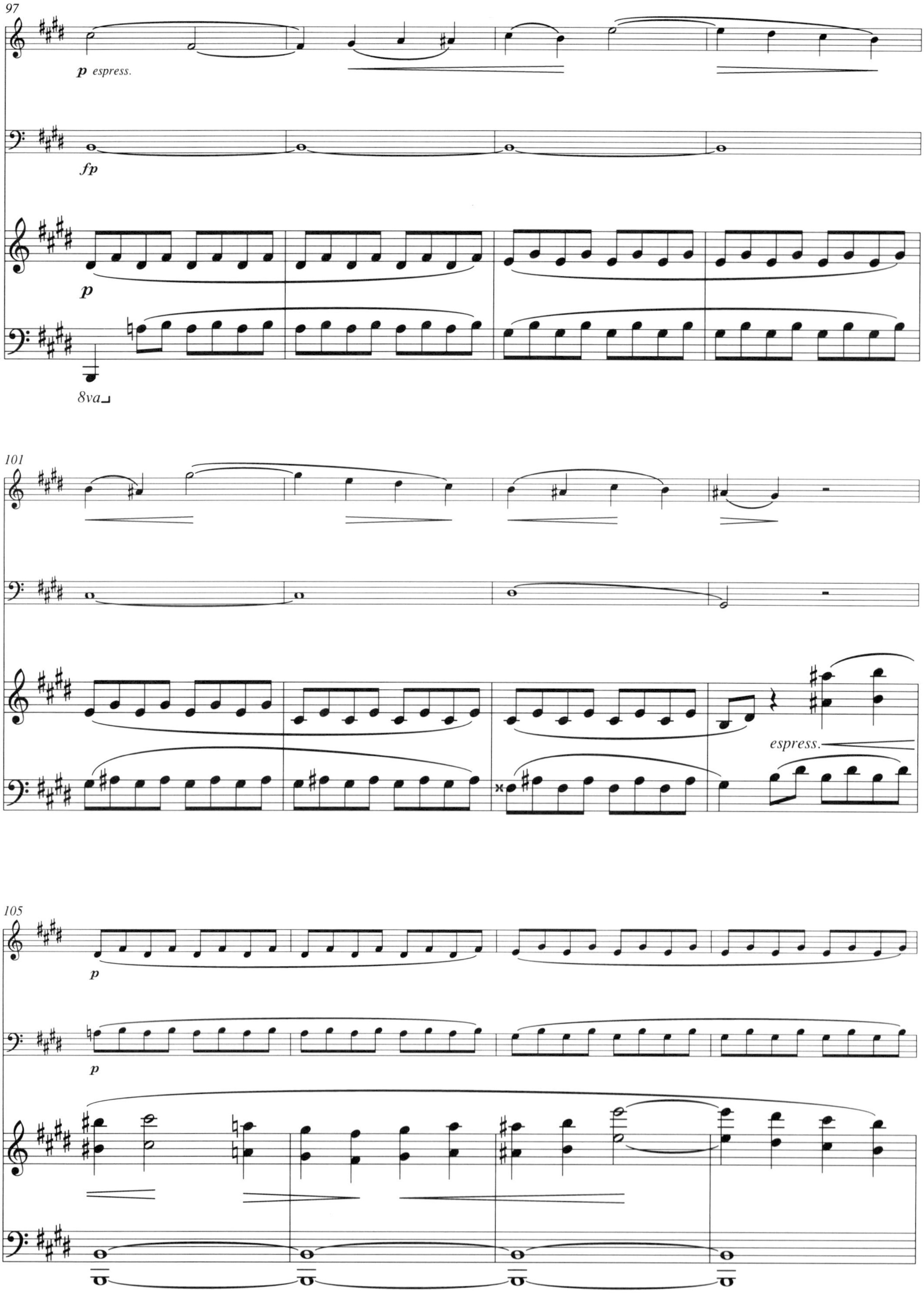
97
p espress.
fp
p
8va
101
espress.
105
p
p

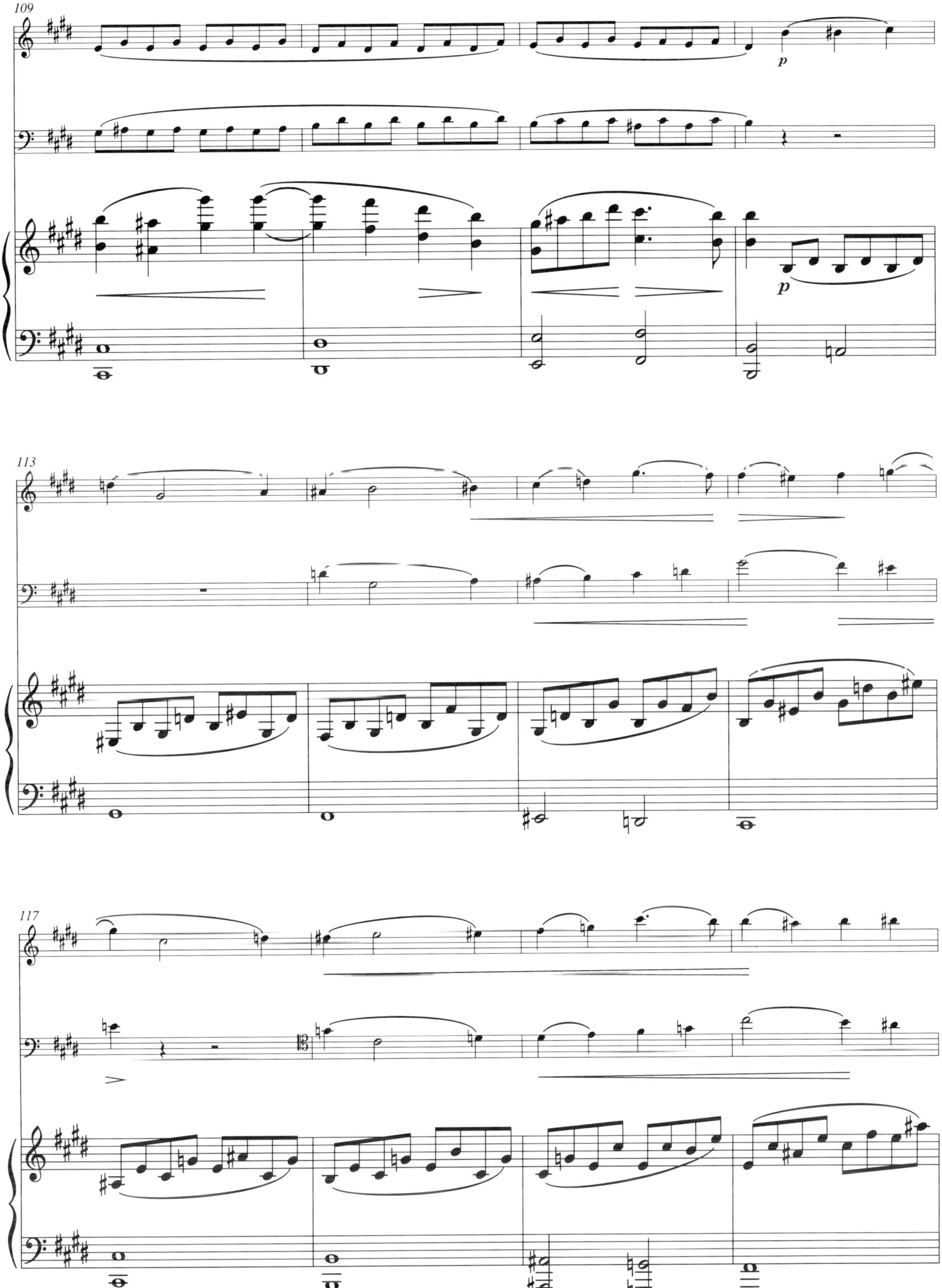
109
p
p
113
117

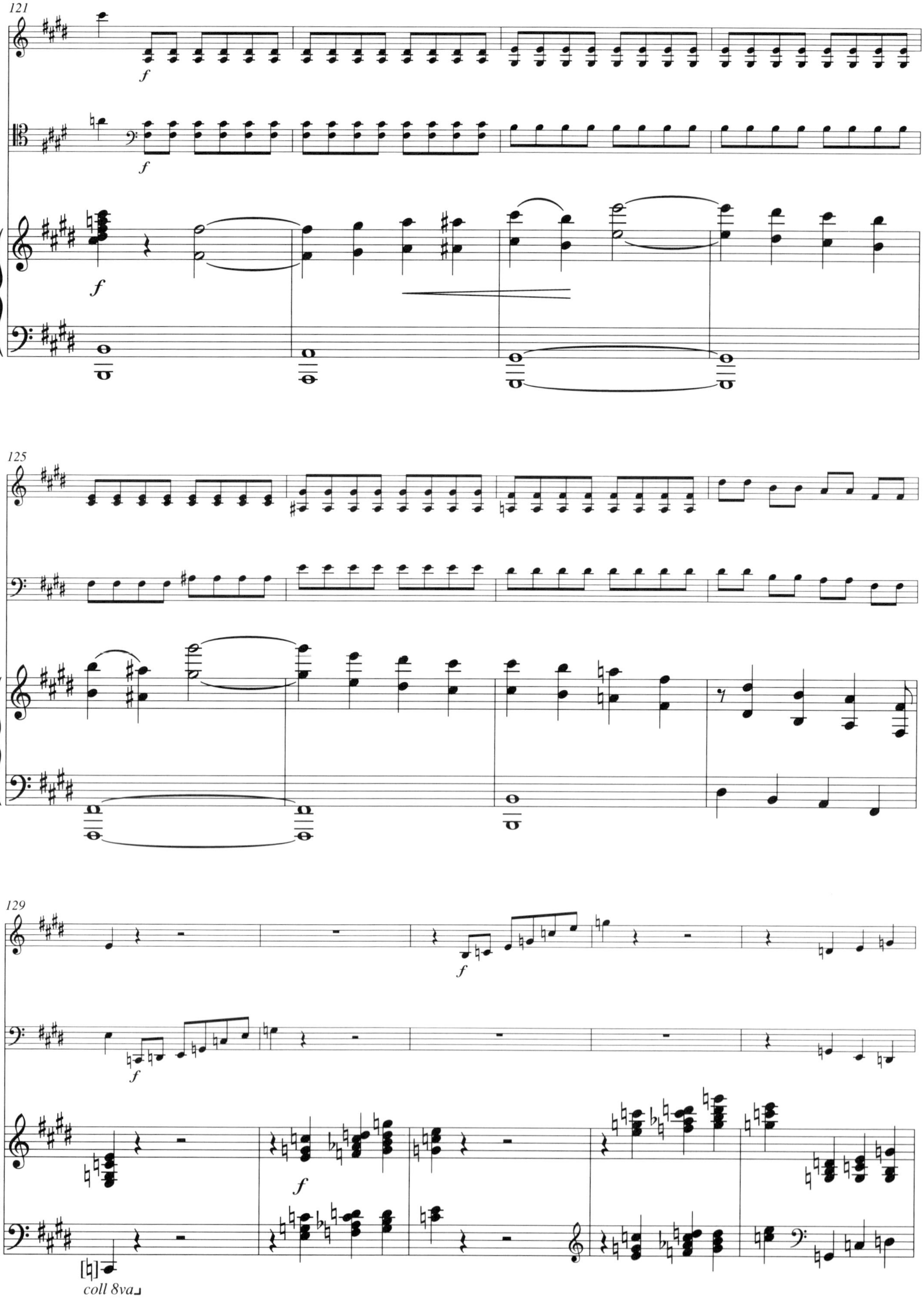
121
f
f
f
125
129
f
f
f
[♮]
coll 8va

101

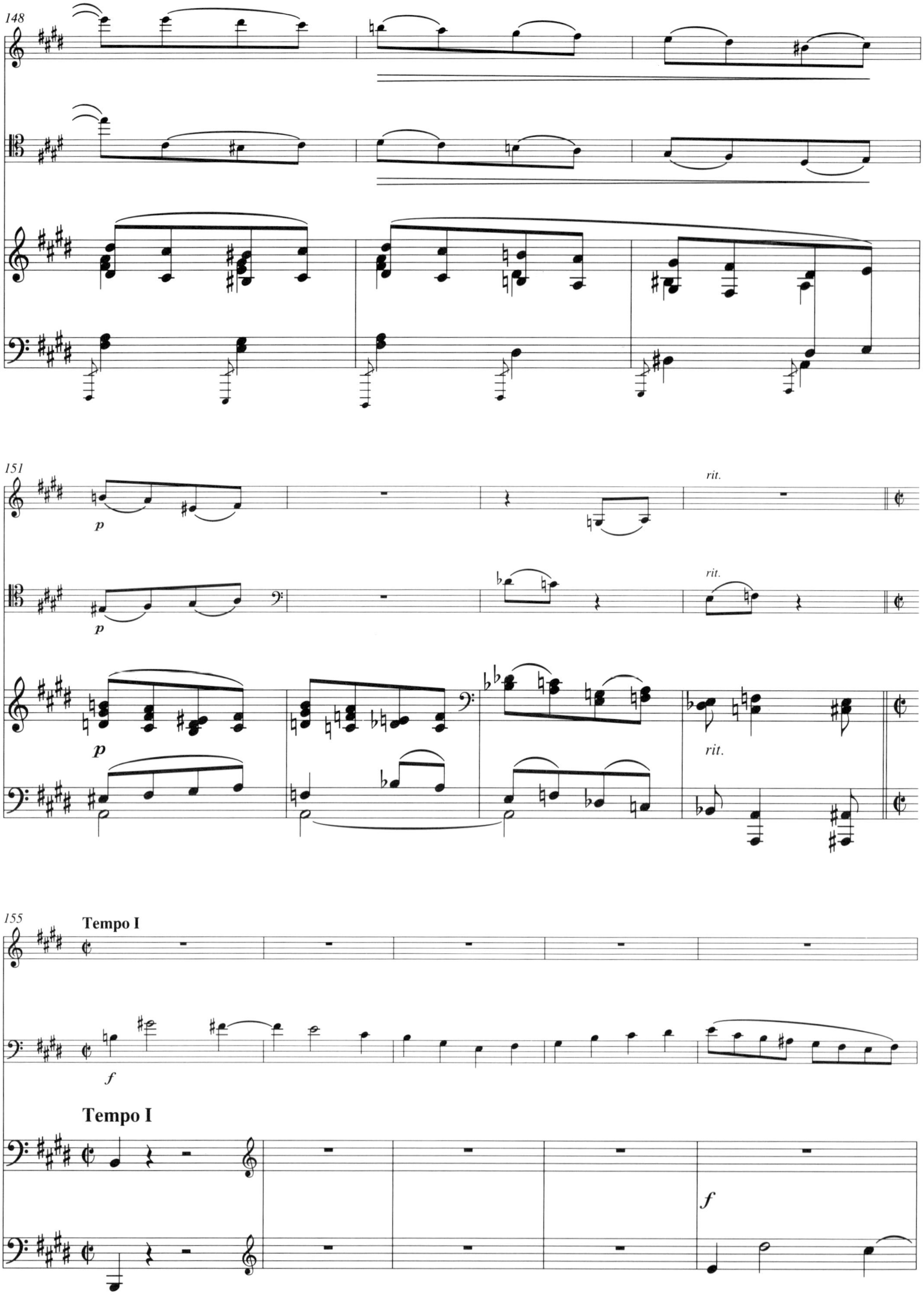
148
151
p
p
p
rit.
rit.
rit.
155
Tempo I
Tempo I
f
f

103

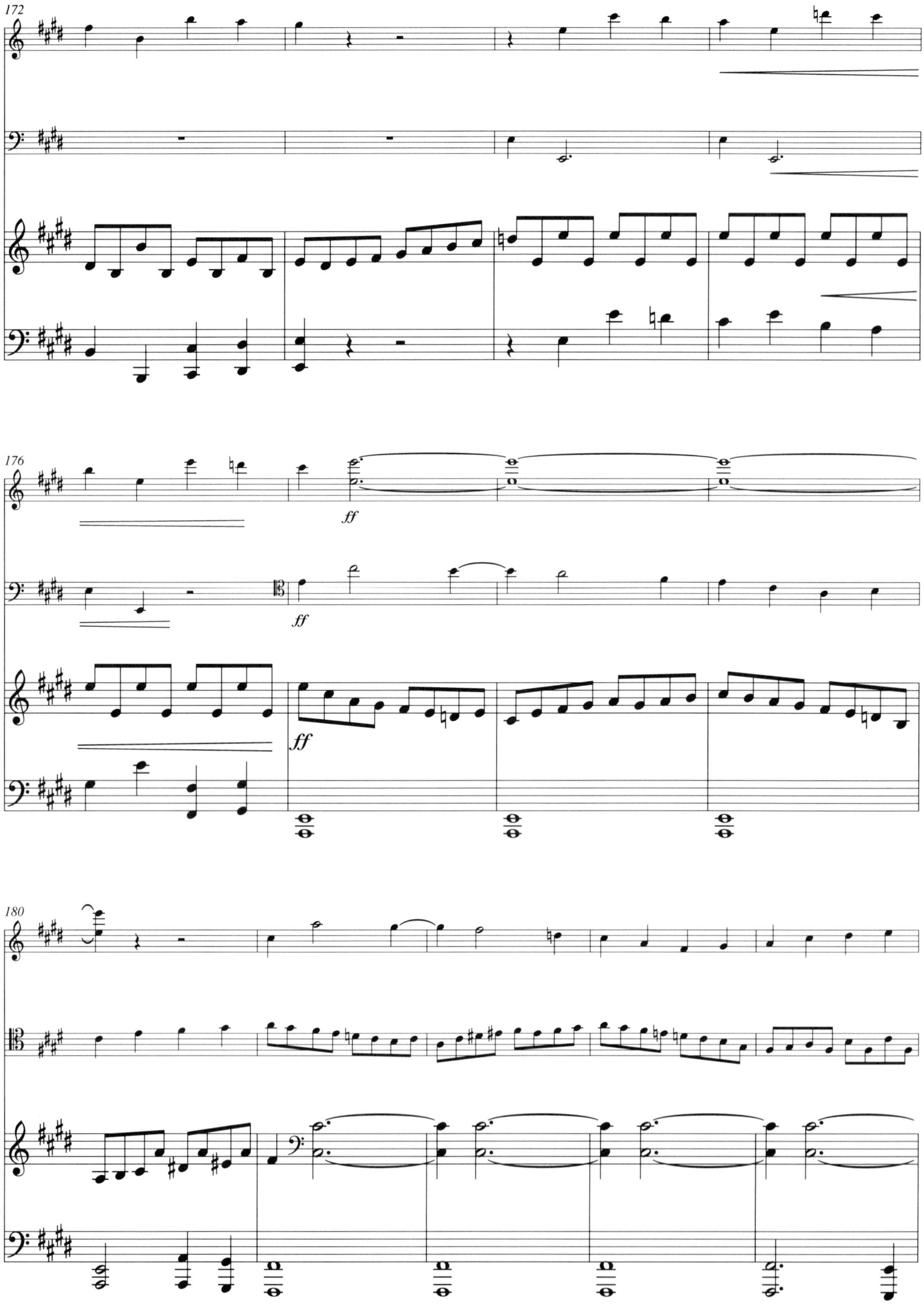
172
176
ff
ff
ff
180

185
ff
ff
ff
189
string.
mf cresc.
string.
mf cresc.
string.
193
mf appass.
f
ff
mf
ff p

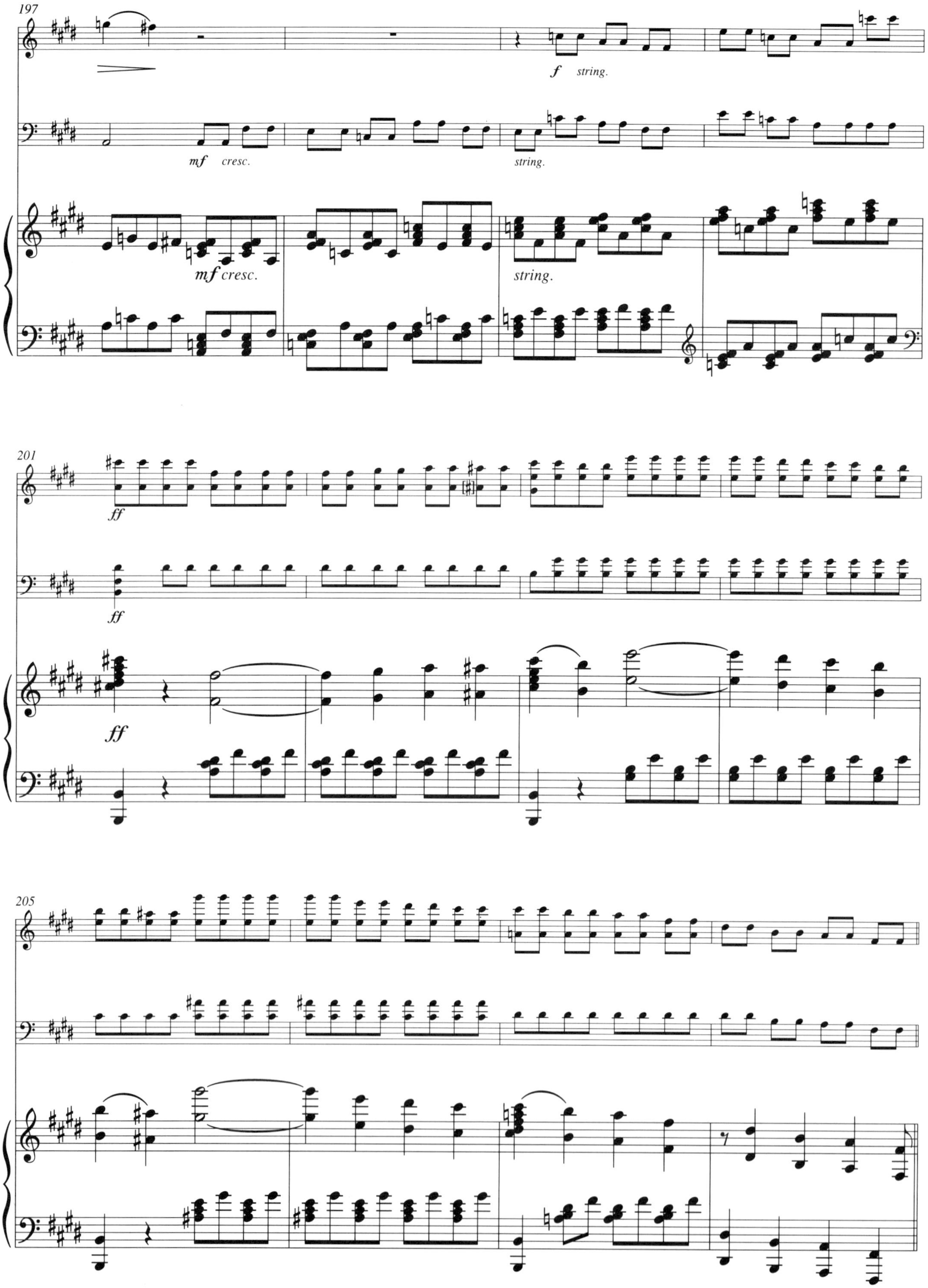
197
mf cresc.
string.
f string.
mf cresc.
string.
201
ff
ff
ff
205

Vivacissimo
209
ff
ff
Vivacissimo
ff
213
f
mf
cresc. poco a poco
217
f cresc. e string.
f string.
f string.

221
8va
224
Prestissimo
ff al fine
ff al fine
Prestissimo
(8va)
ff al fine
229

Sonata, Op. 6

[I]

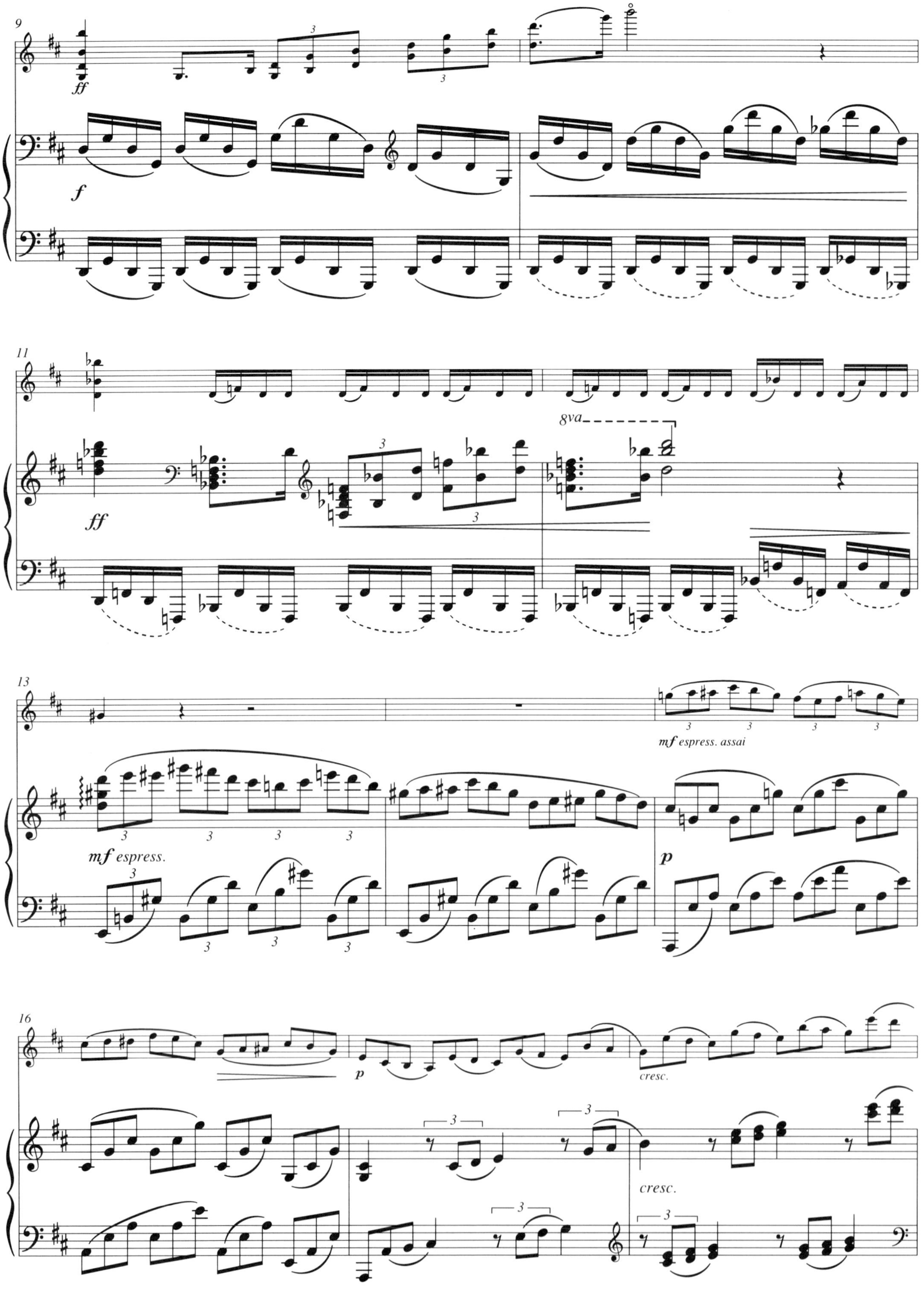
ff
f
ff
8va
mf espress. assai
mf espress.
p
p
cresc.
cresc.

111

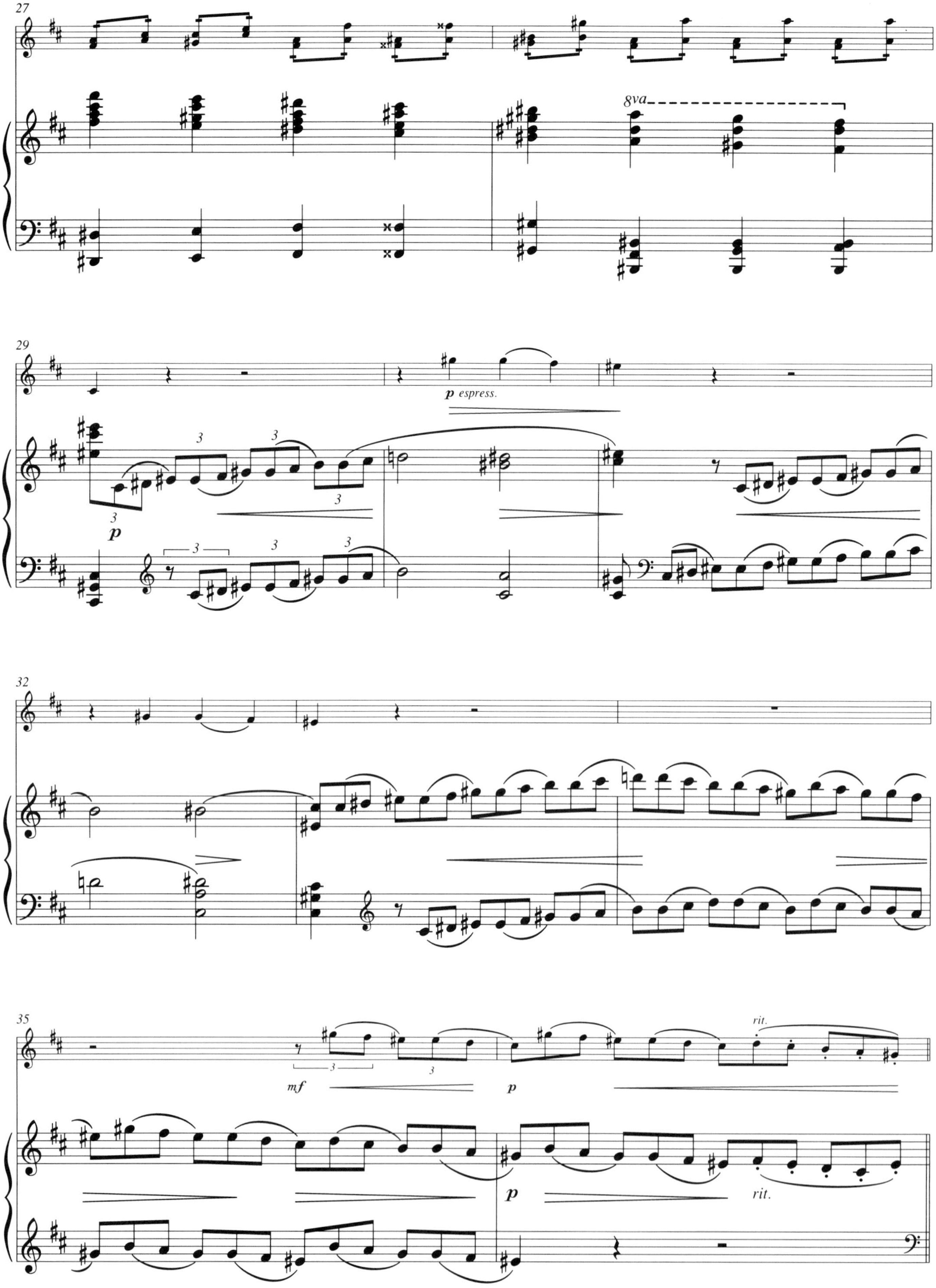
27
8va
29
p espress.
p
32
35
mf
p
rit.
p
rit.

37
Un poco meno mosso ♩ = 100
p cantando
40
rit.
a tempo
p
rit.
a tempo
43
smorz.
rit.
a tempo
rit.
a tempo
mf
46

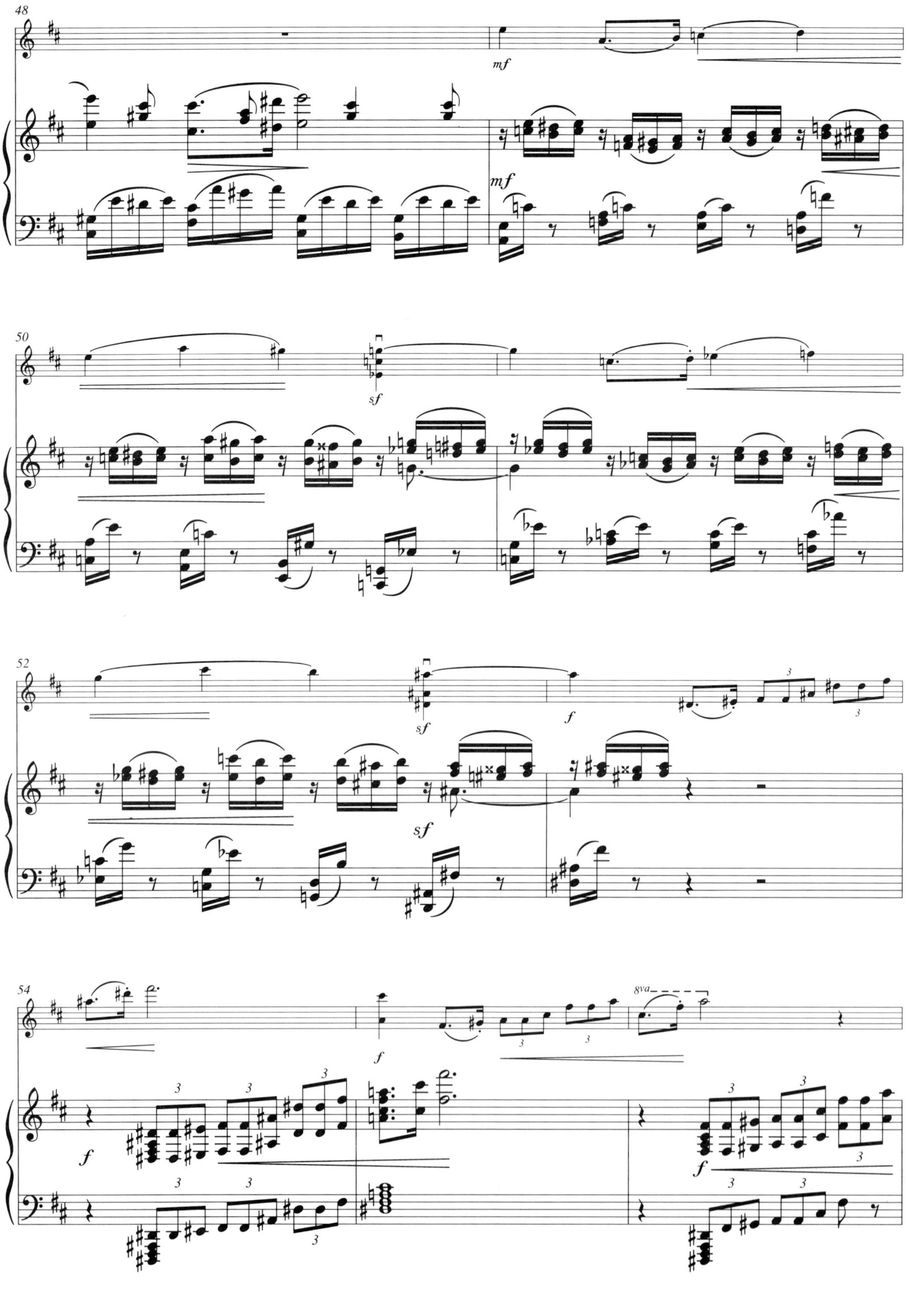
48
mf
mf
50
sf
52
sf
sf
f
54
f
8va
f
f

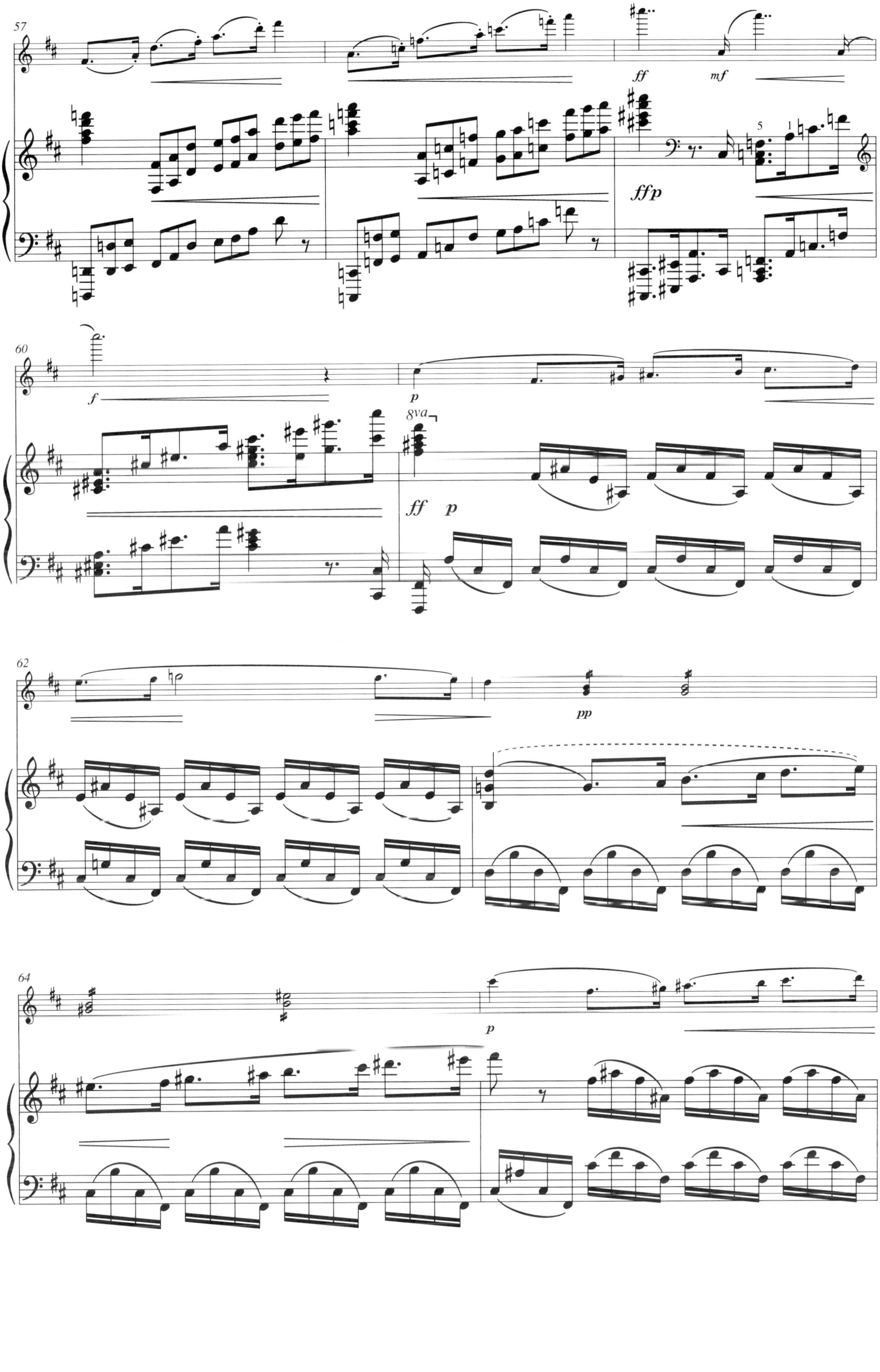
57
ff
mf
ffp
60
f
p
8va
ff
p
62
pp
64
p

116

75
f
f
f
78
2.
pizz.
p
8va
pp legatissimo
80
arco
p
8va
82
pizz.
(8va)
sempre pp

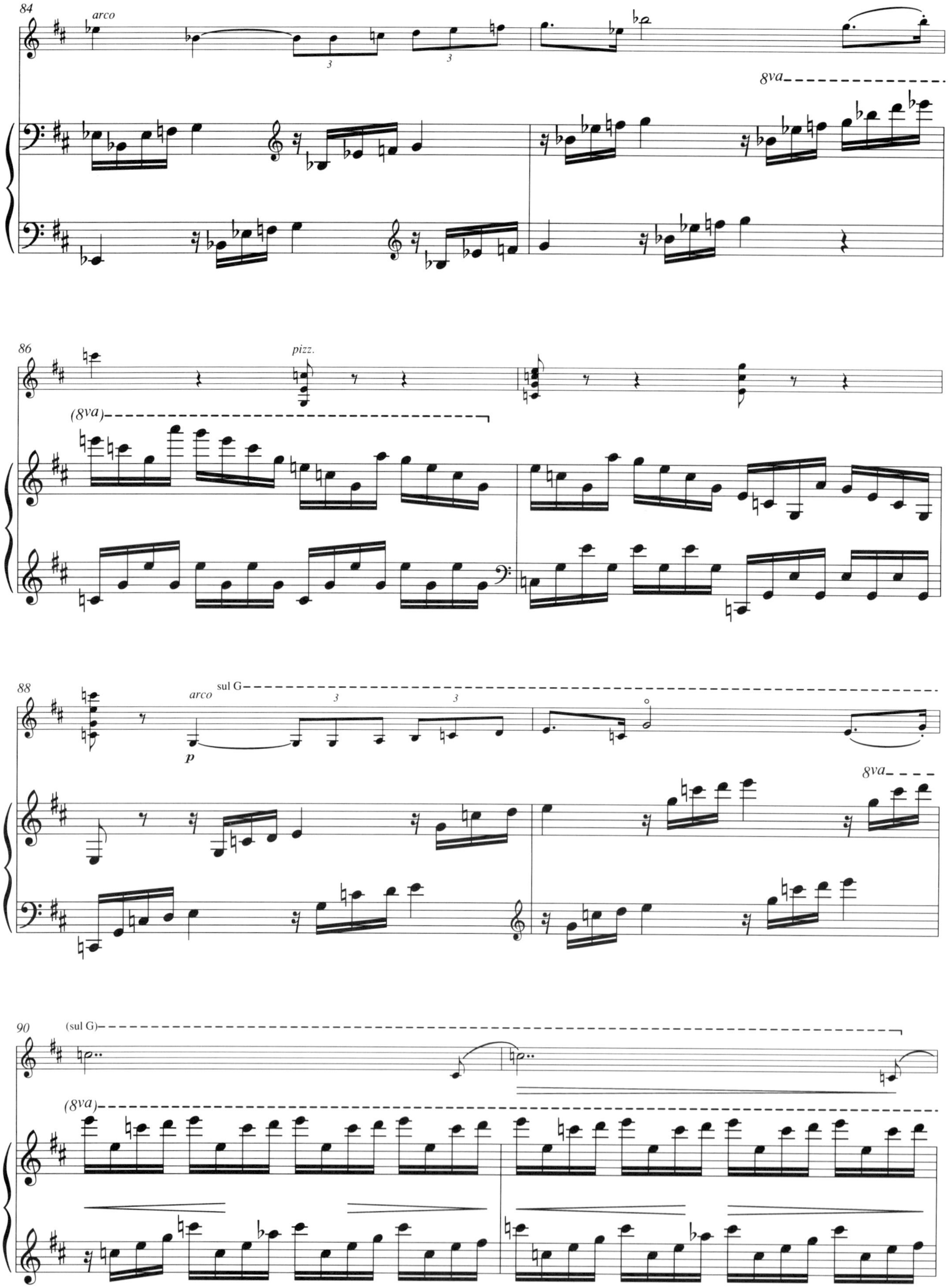
84
arco
3
3
8va
86
pizz.
(8va)
88
arco
sul G
3
3
p
8va
90
(sul G)
(8va)

92
pochiss. rit.
(8va)
pochiss. rit.
94
a tempo
pp
3
3
(8va)
a tempo
ppp
96
8va
4
98
(8va)

100
pizz.
8va
pp sostenuto
8va
104
arco
p sostenuto
8va
109
mf
mf
112

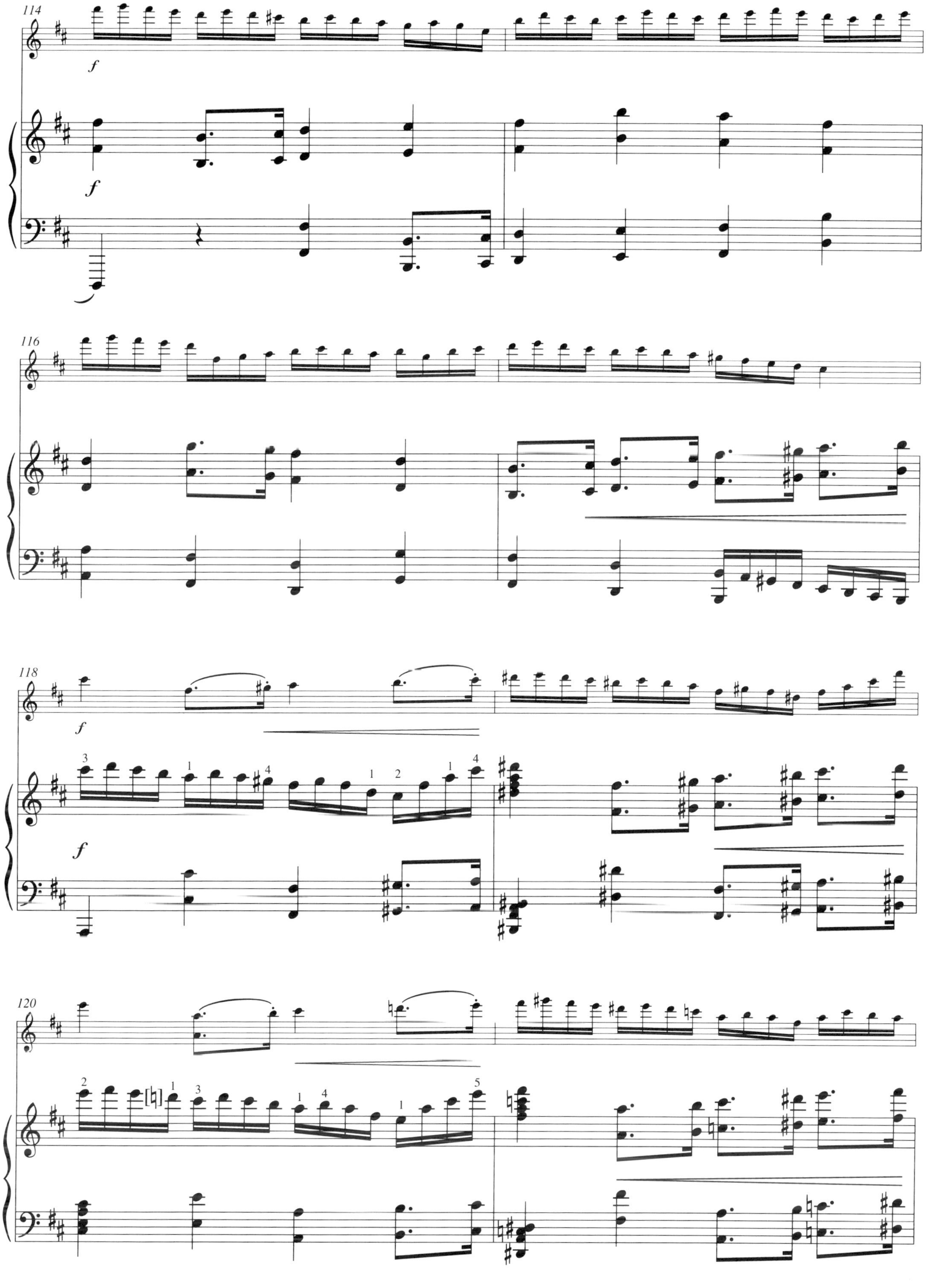
114
f
f
116
118
f
f
120

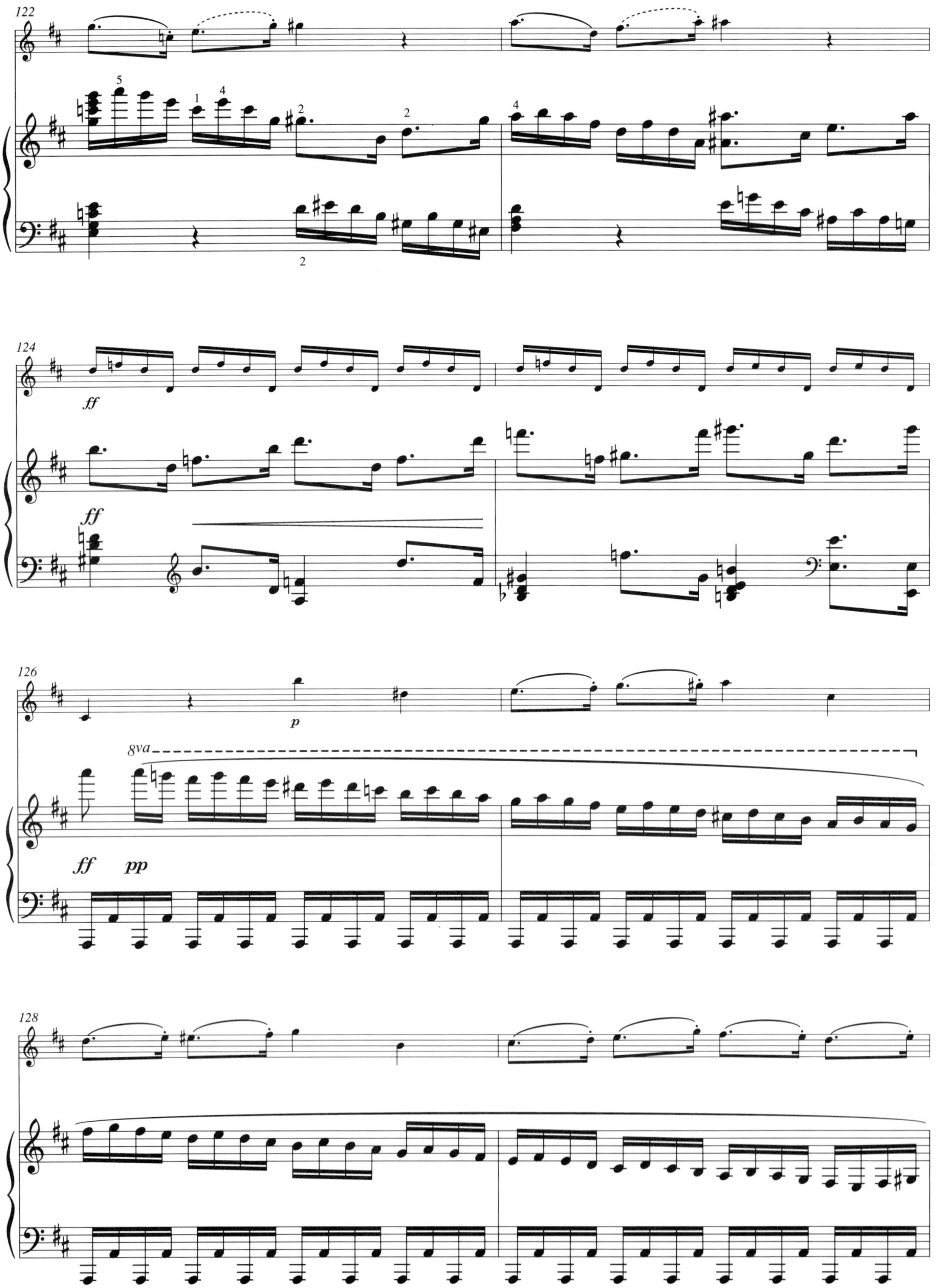
122
124
ff
ff
126
p
8va
ff
pp
128

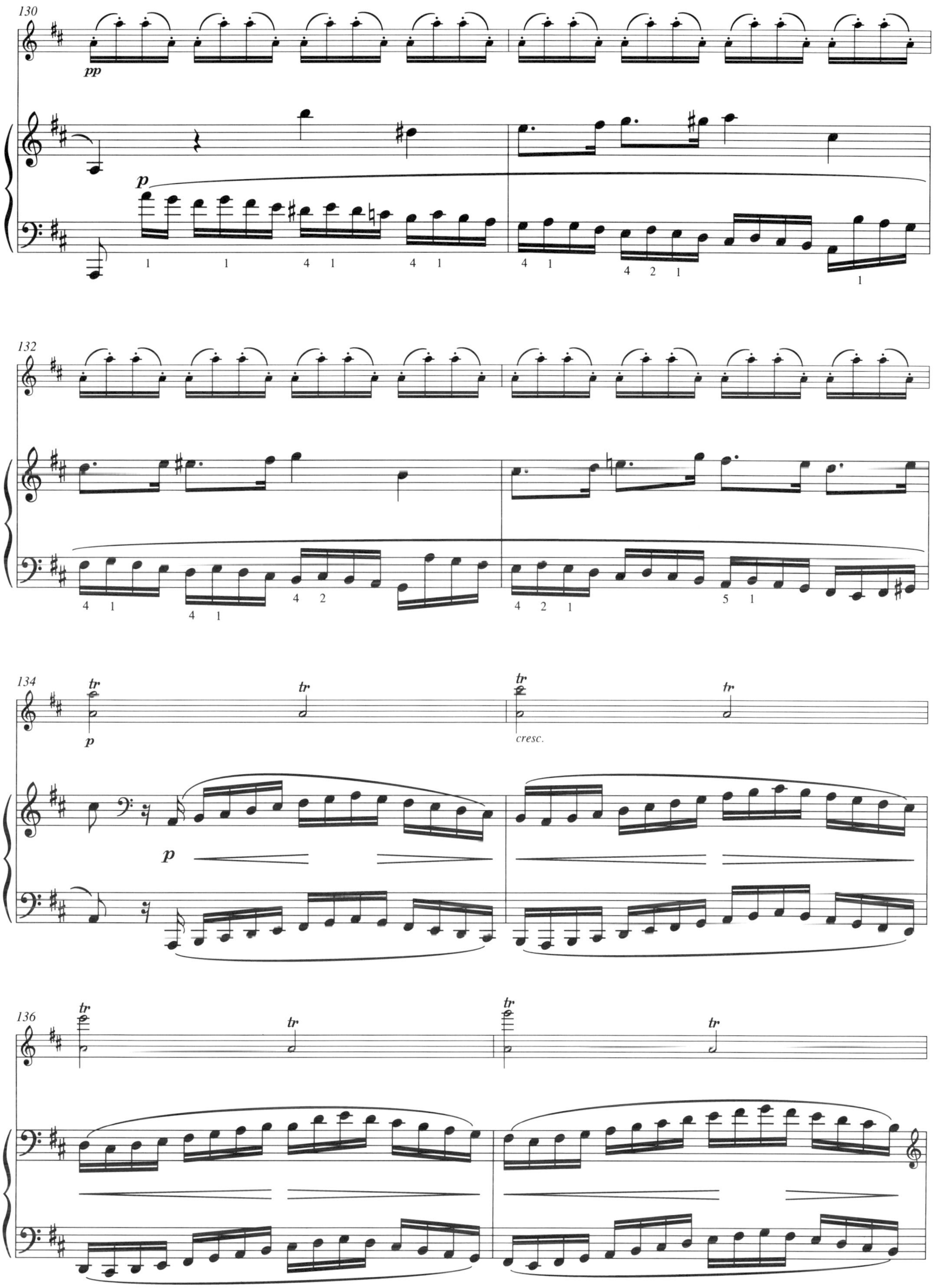
130
pp
p
132
134
tr
p
cresc.
136

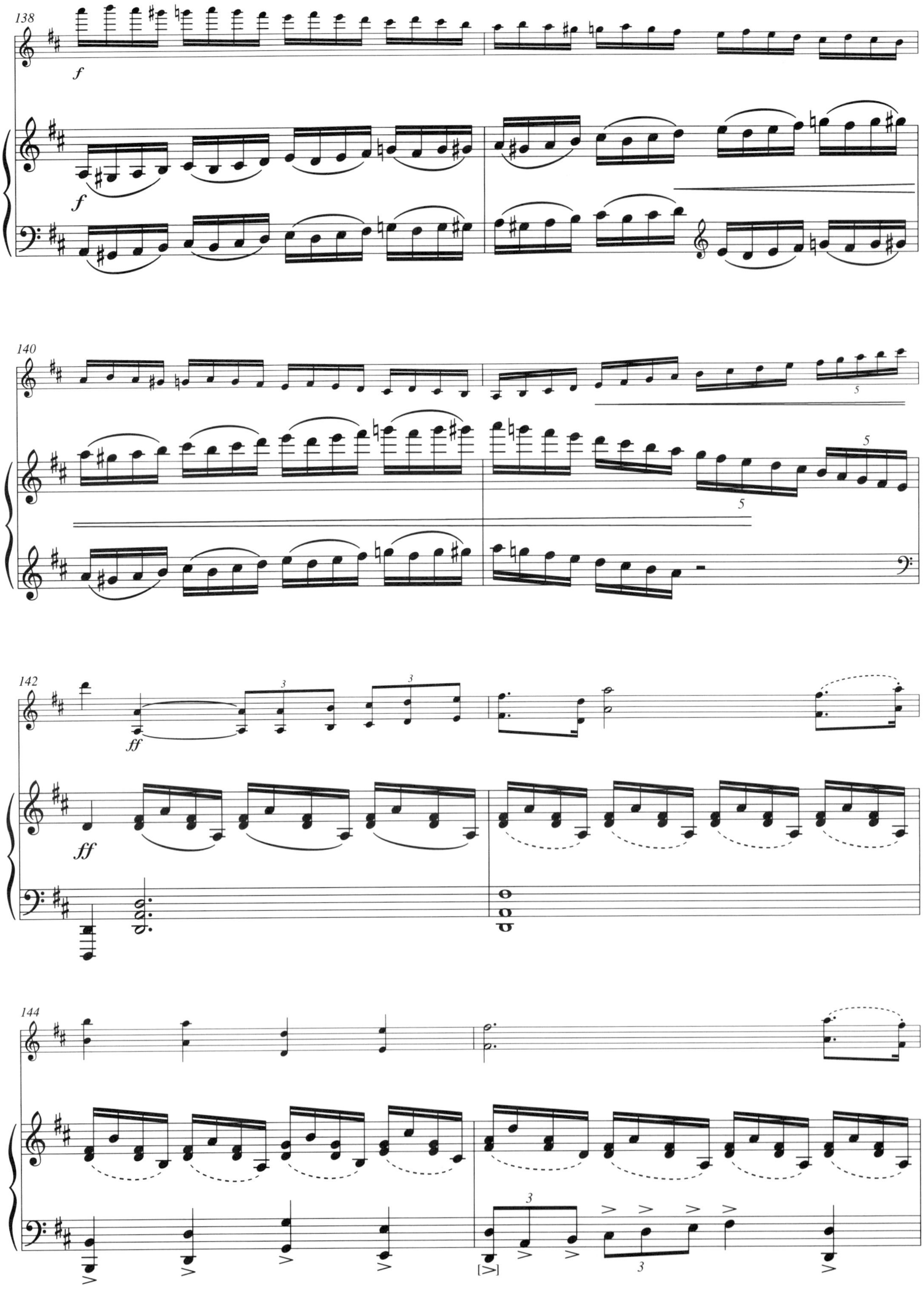
138
f
f
140
142
ff
ff
144

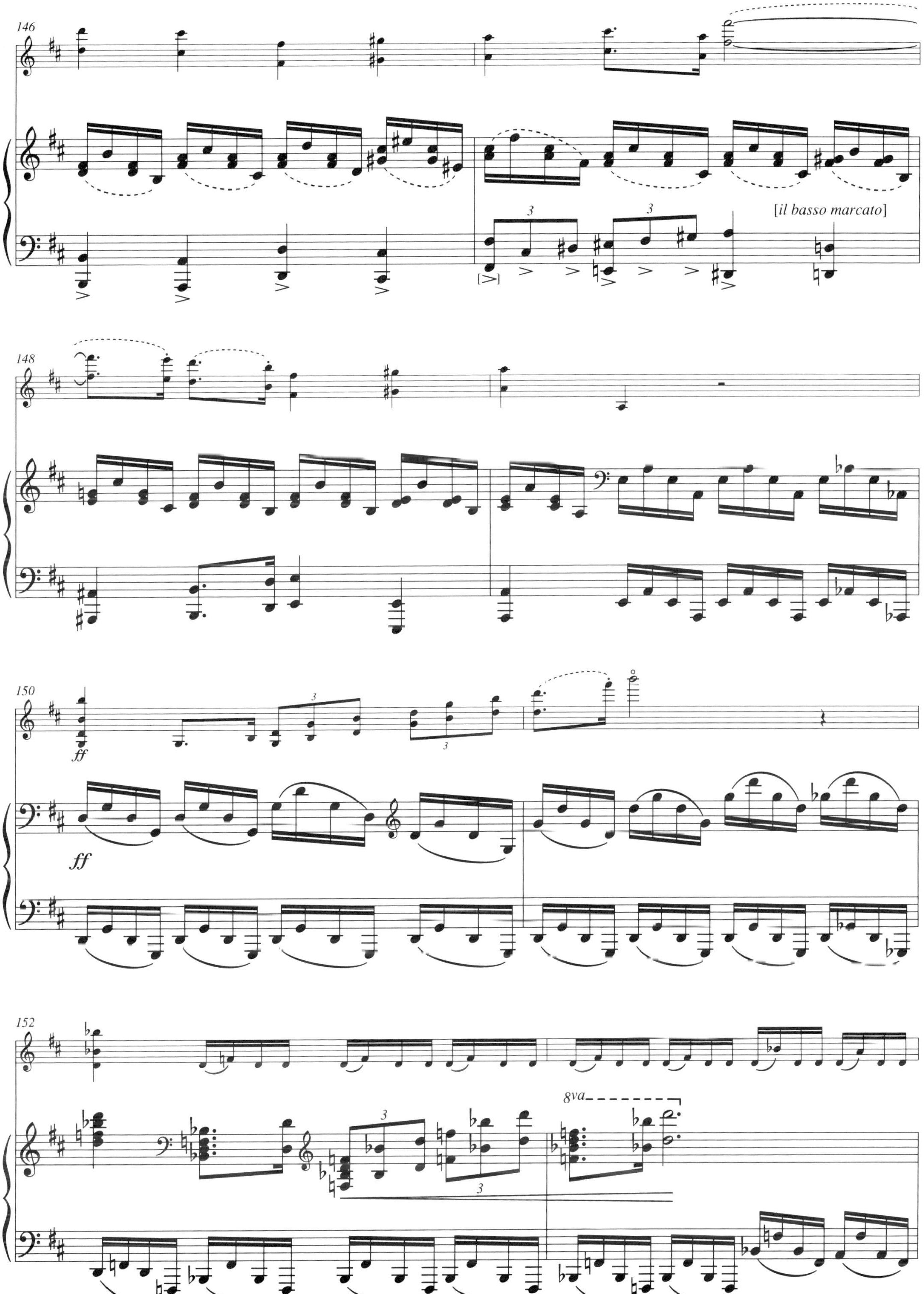
146
[il basso marcato]
148
150
ff
ff
152
8va

154
mf espress. assai
156
p espress. assai
p
159
p espress.
p
163
p
rit.
rit.

166
Un poco meno mosso
rit.
cantando
rit.
170
a tempo
p
rit.
smorz.
a tempo
p
rit.
coll 8va
174
a tempo
a tempo
176
[rit.]
rit.

178
a tempo
mf
sf
mf a tempo
180
sf
f
182
f
3
f
coll 8va
185
coll 8va
8va

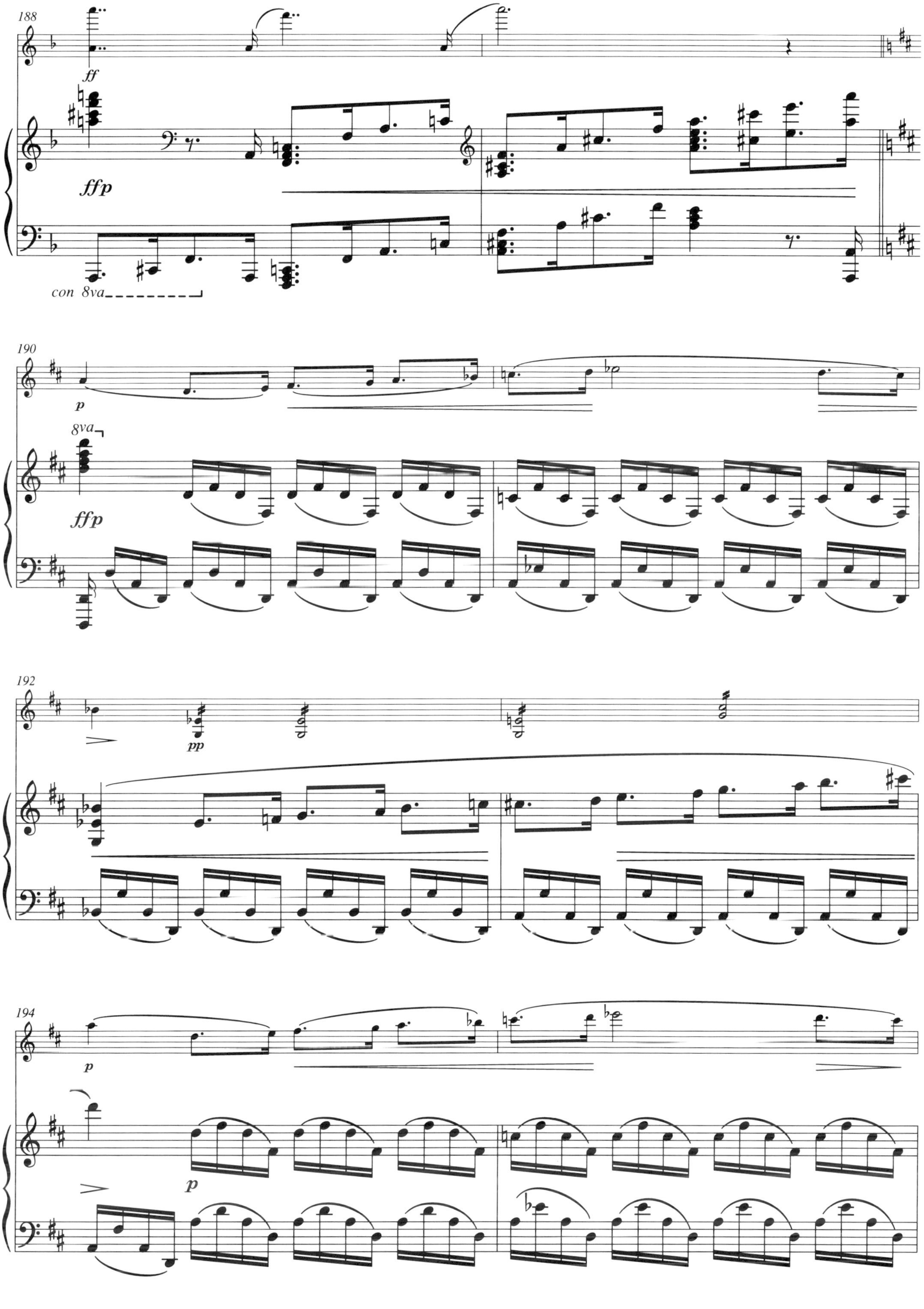
188
ff
ffp
con 8va
190
p
8va
ffp
192
pp
194
p
p

196
8va
198
pizz.
p
(8va)
pp legatissimo
200
arco
p
3
3
8va
202
pizz.
(8va)
pp sempre

204
arco
3
3
8va
206
pizz.
(8va)
208
arco
sul G
3
3
sul D
8va
210
(sul D)
sul G
(8va)
pp

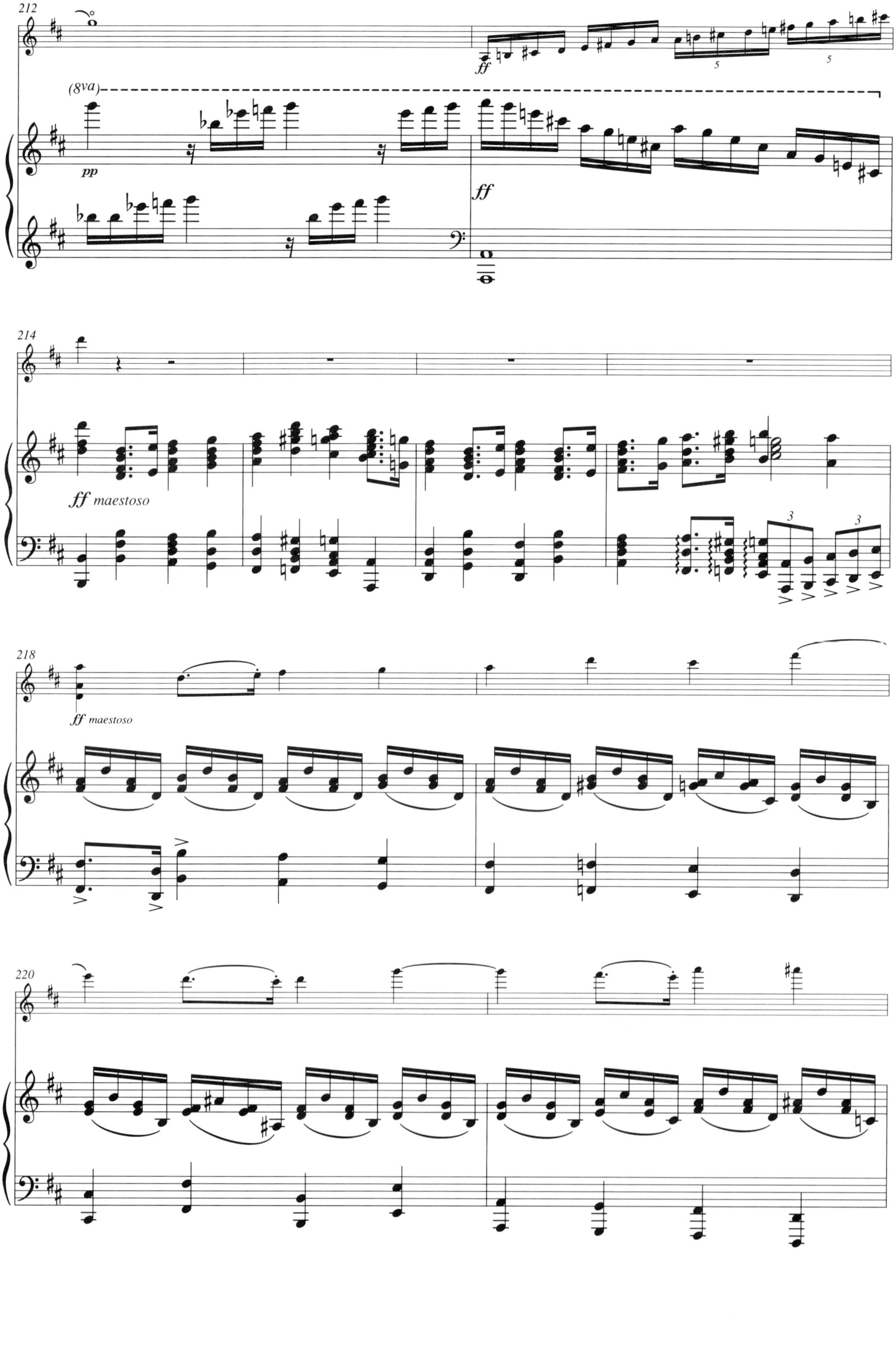
212
(8va)
pp
ff
5
5
ff
214
ff maestoso
3
3
218
ff maestoso
220

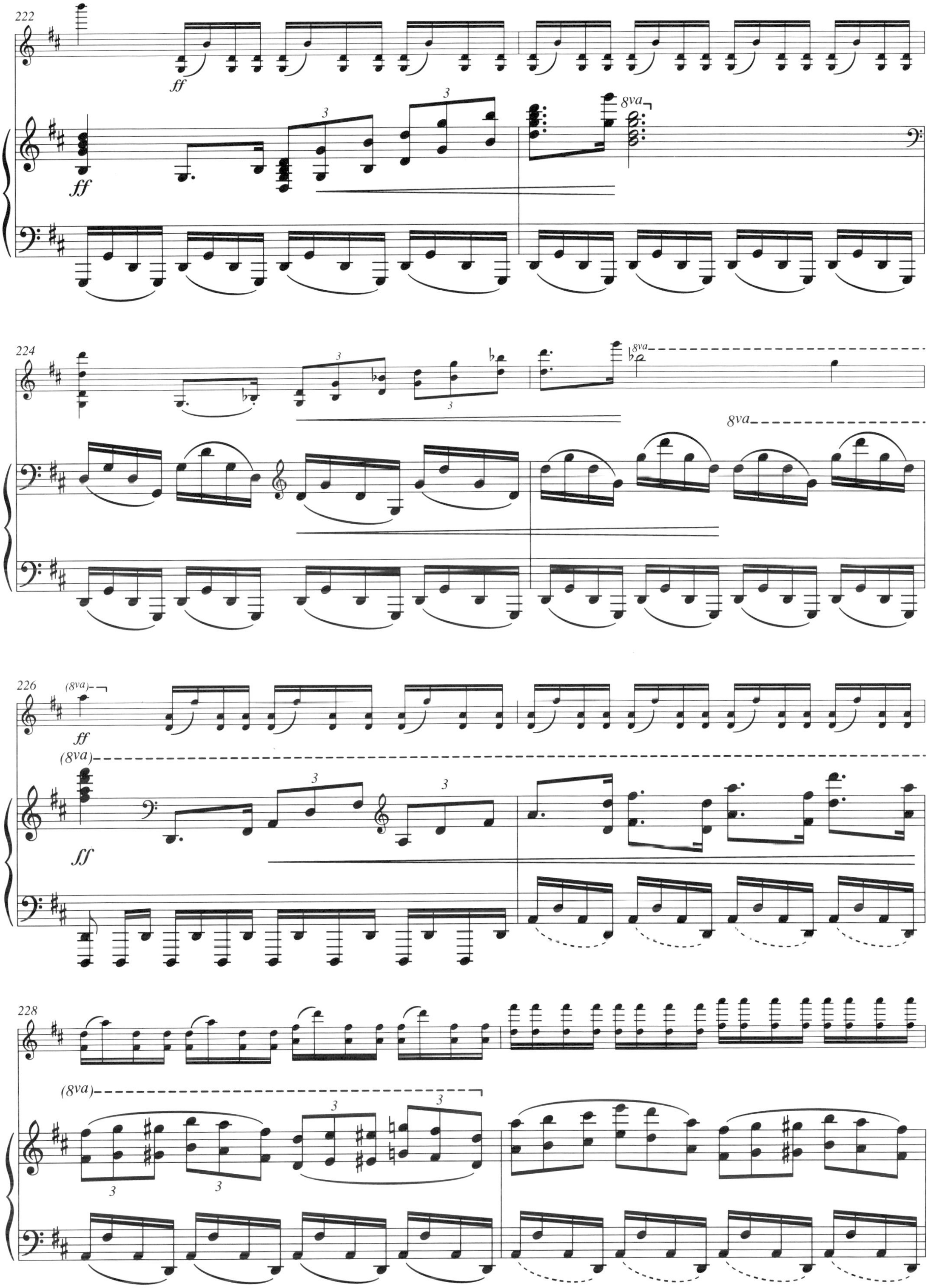
222
ff
ff
8va
224
8va
8va
226
(8va)
ff
(8va)
ff
228
(8va)

230
8va
3
fff al fine
3
fff al fine
3
3
3
3
coll 8va
232
(coll 8va)
235

[II]

Adagio con espressione

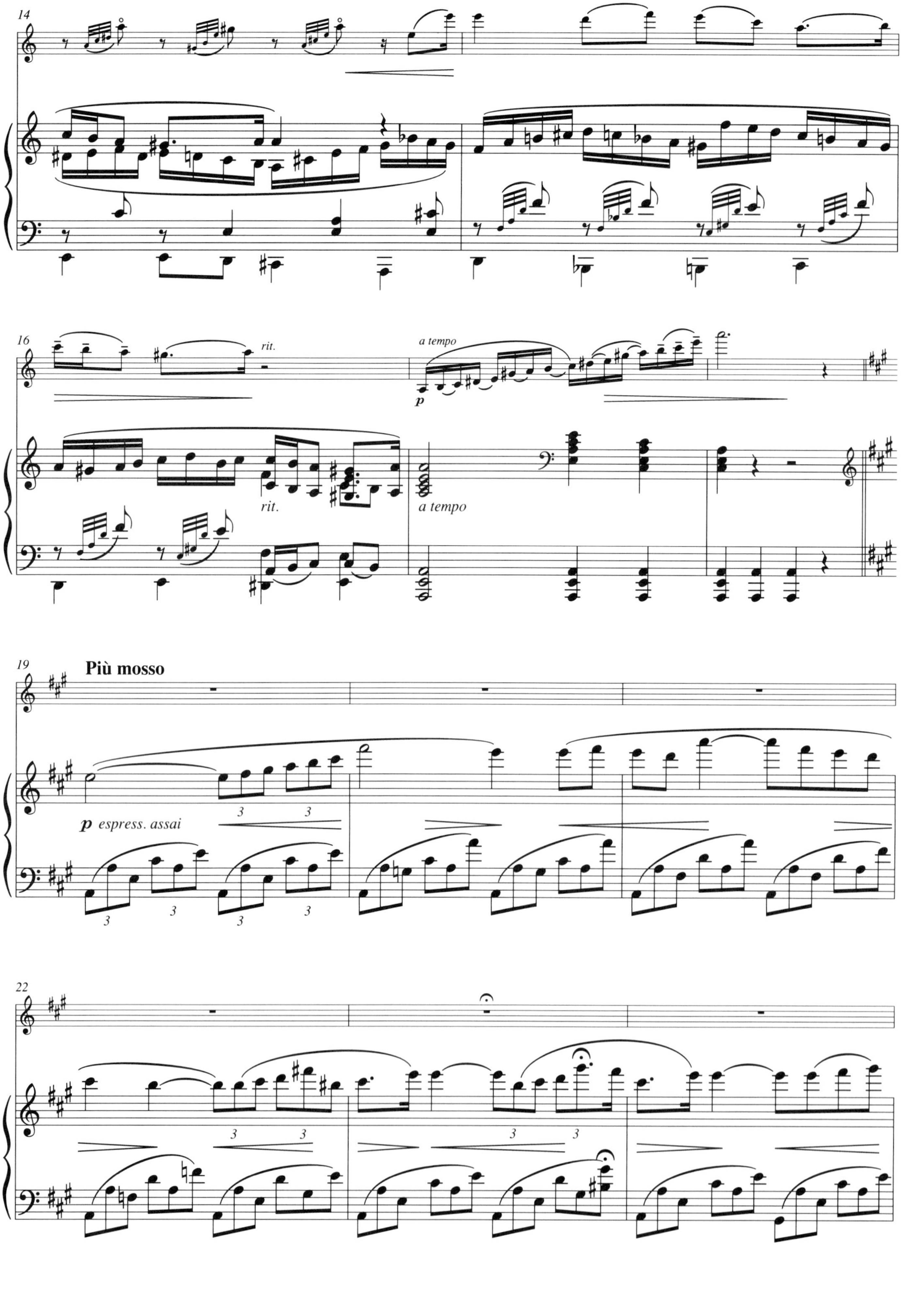
14
16
rit.
a tempo
p
rit.
a tempo
19
Più mosso
p espress. assai
3
22

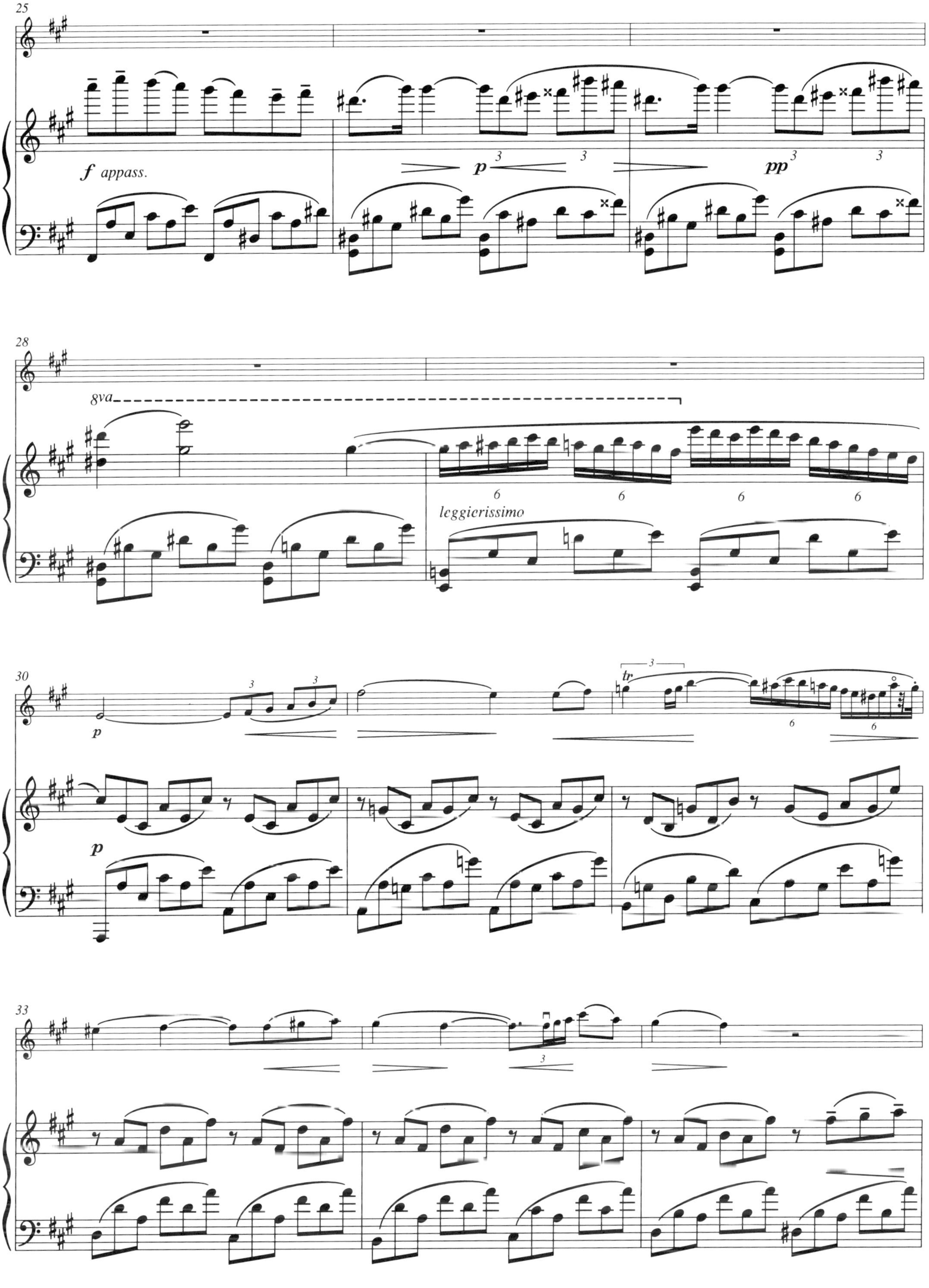
25
f appass.
p
pp
28
8va
leggierissimo
30
p
tr
33

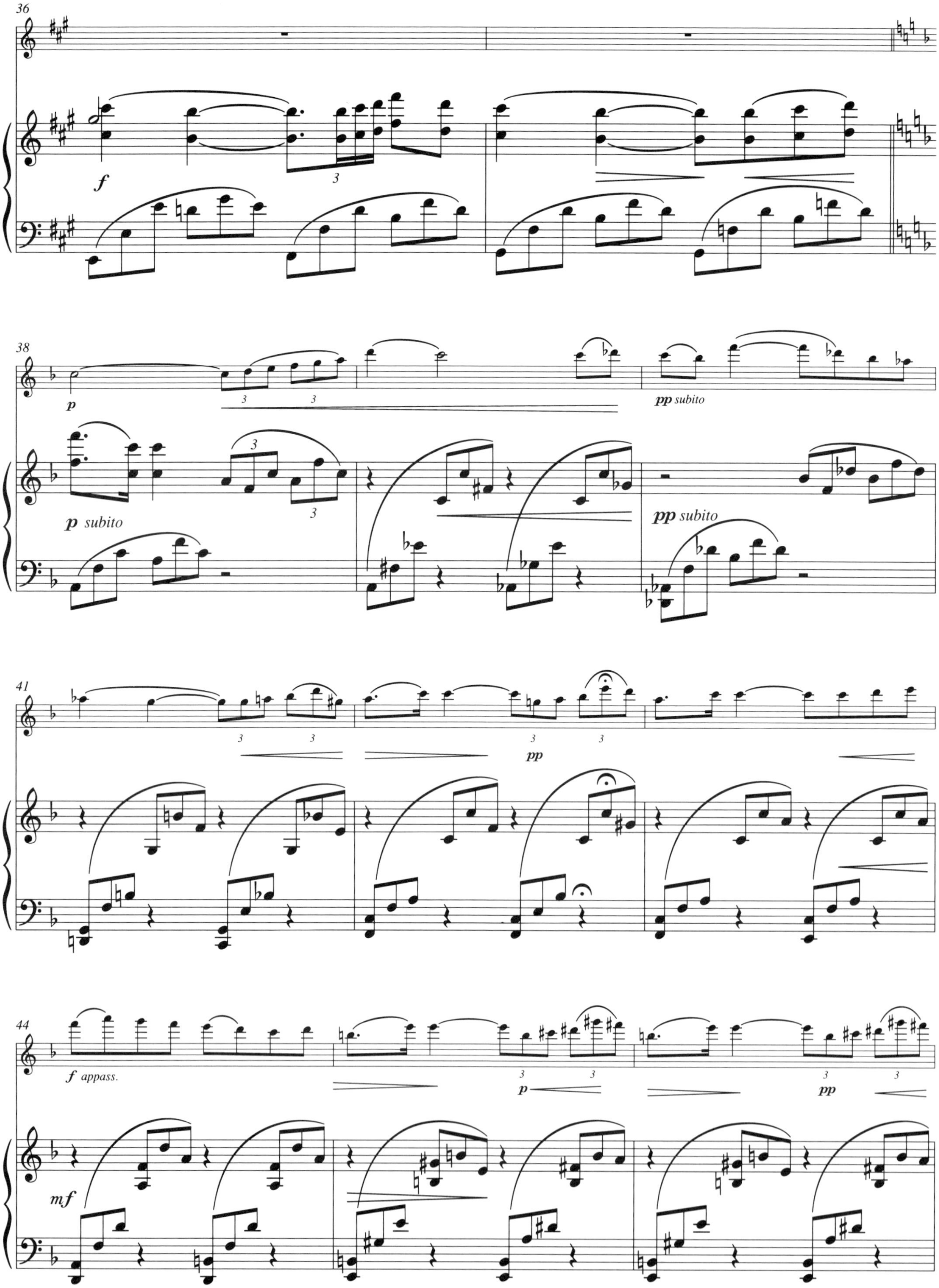
36
f
38
p
p subito
pp subito
41
pp
44
f appass.
mf
p
pp

139

59
espress.
tr
mf
p
pp
8va
63
p
pp
p espress.
66
rit.
Più mosso
pp
pp rit.
69
Tempo I
pp

[III]

31
8va
8va
3
espr.
38
arco
(8va)
4 5 4 5 4 5
4
3 4 5 4 5
45
sul G
mf espress.
mf
espress.
52
(sul G)
sul D

143

144

102
(8va)
108
sul A
p
(8va)
simile
pp leggierissimo
114
8va
119
(8va)
p
espress.

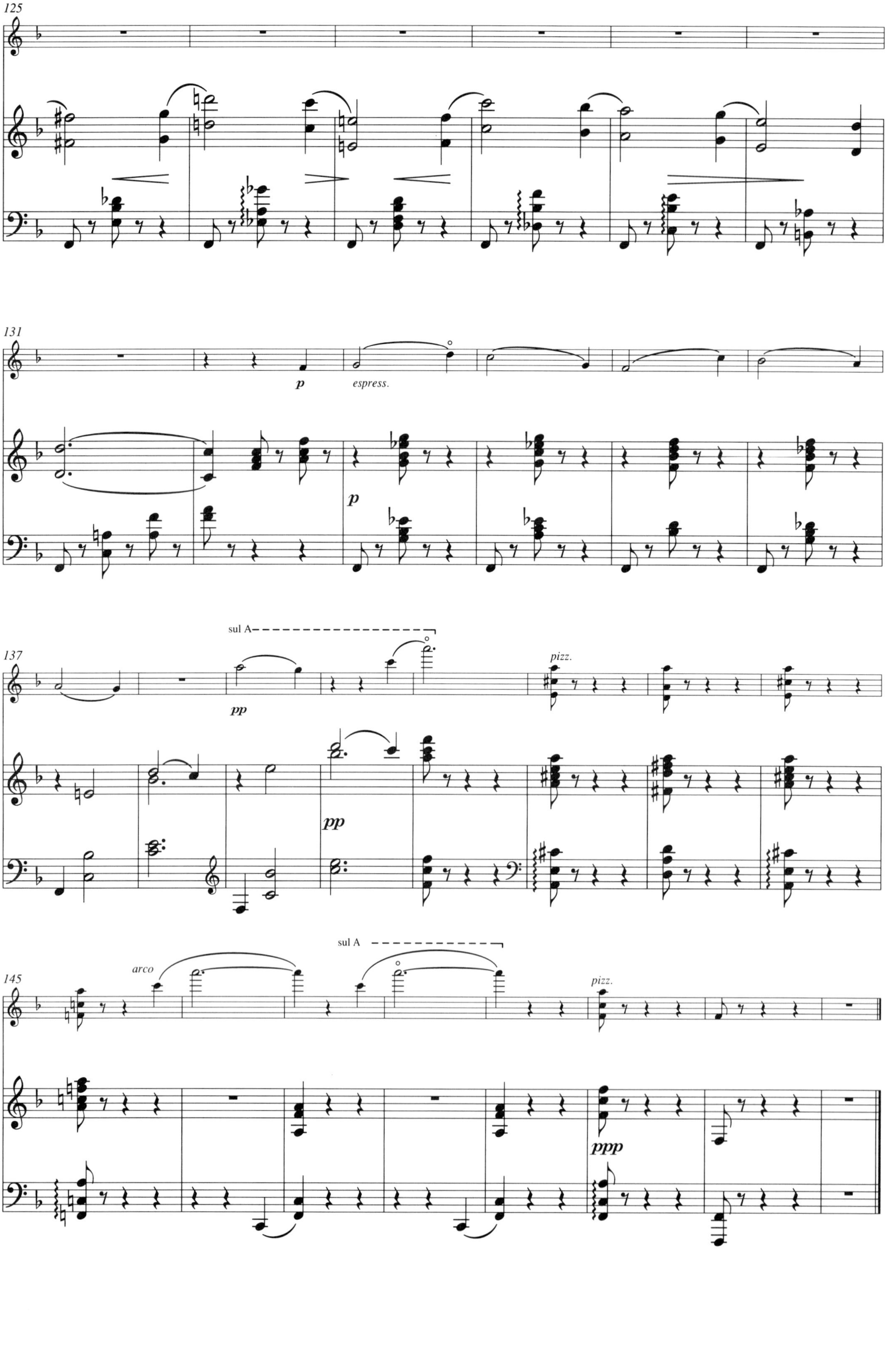
125
131
p
espress.
p
137
sul A
pp
pp
pizz.
145
arco
sul A
pizz.
ppp

[IV]

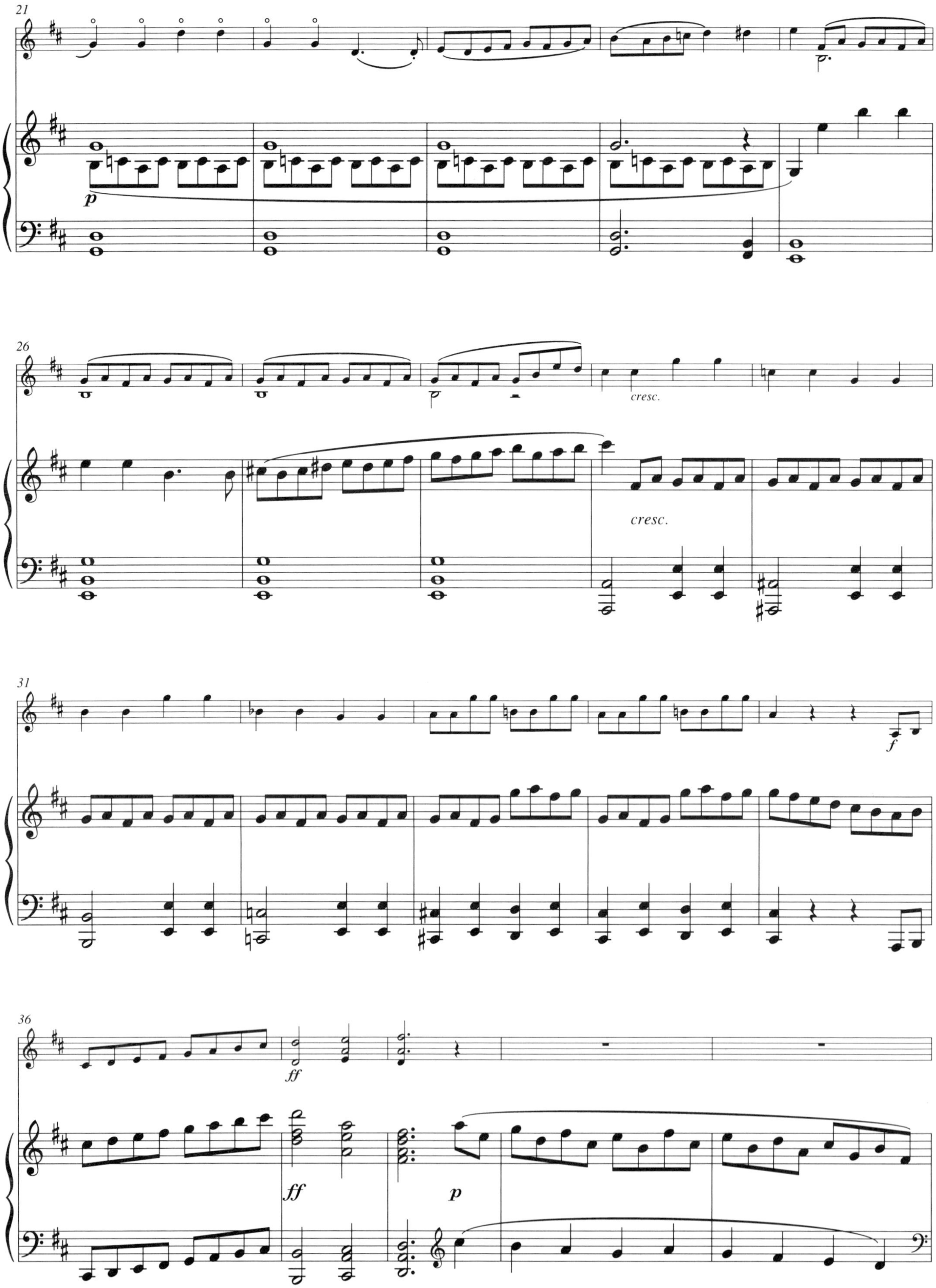
21
p
26
cresc.
cresc.
31
f
36
ff
ff
p

149

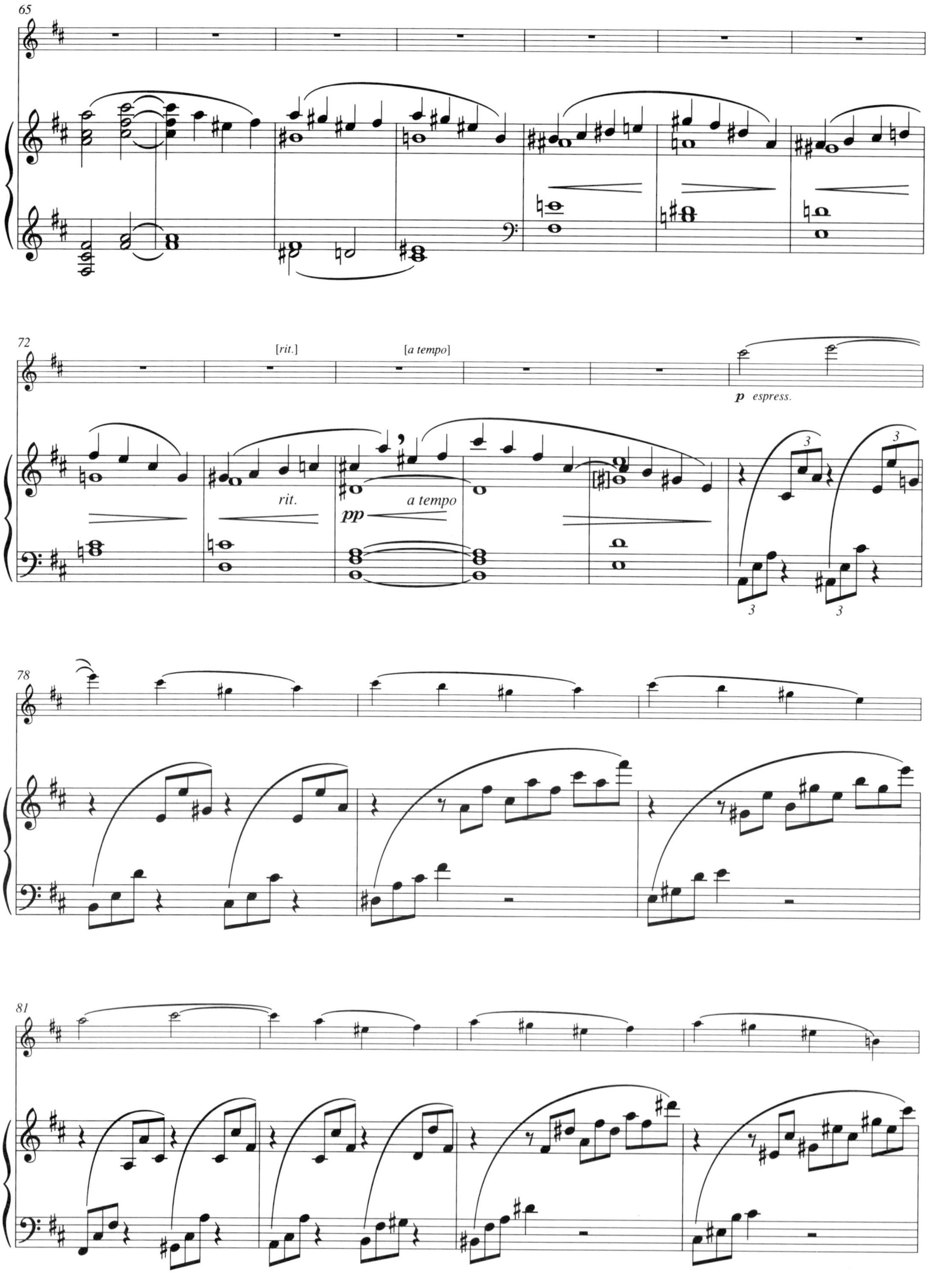
65
72
[rit.]
[a tempo]
rit.
pp
a tempo
p espress.
78
81

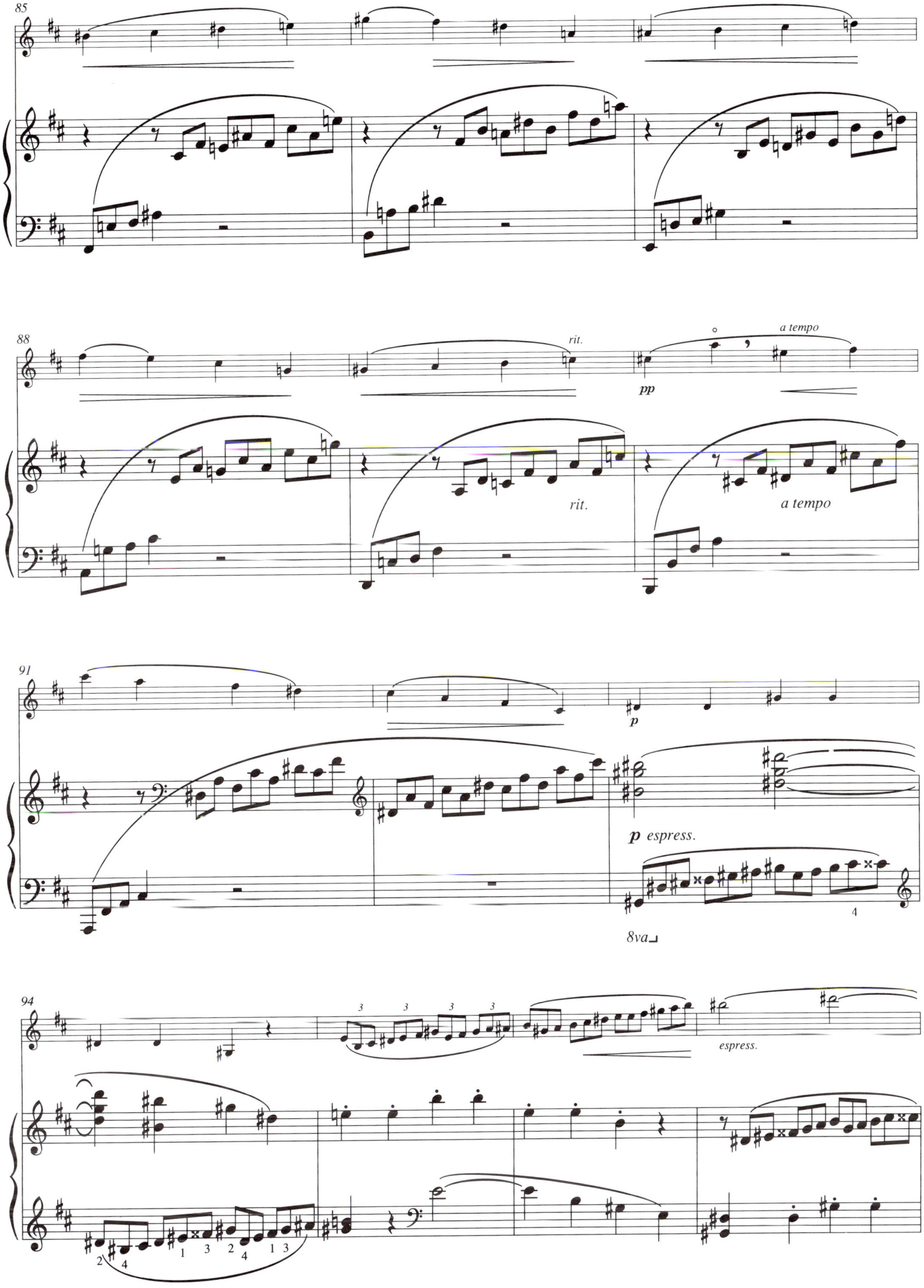
85
88
rit.
a tempo
pp
rit.
a tempo
91
p
p espress.
8va
94
espress.

152

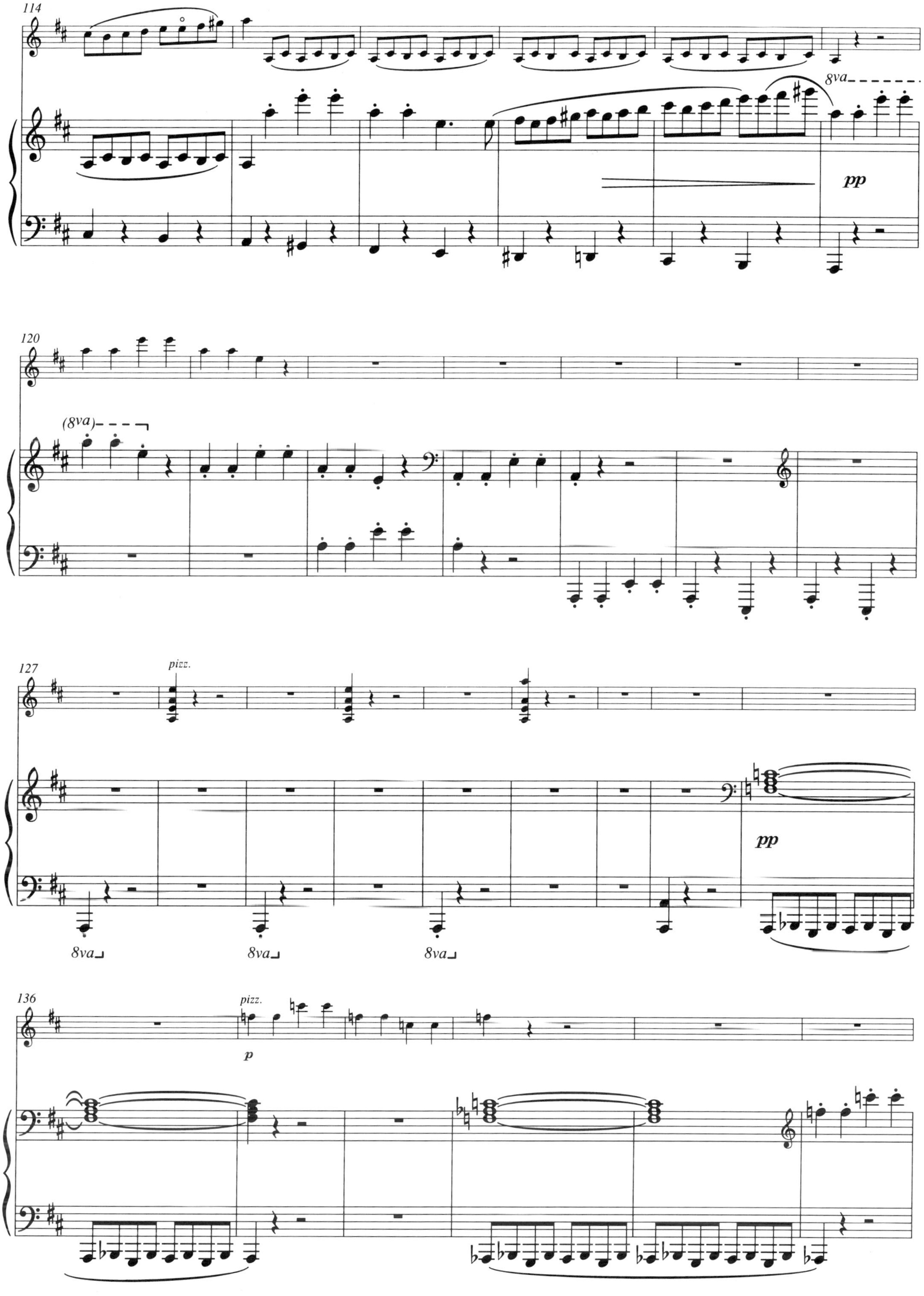
114
8va
pp
120
(8va)
127
pizz.
pp
8va
8va
8va
136
pizz.
p

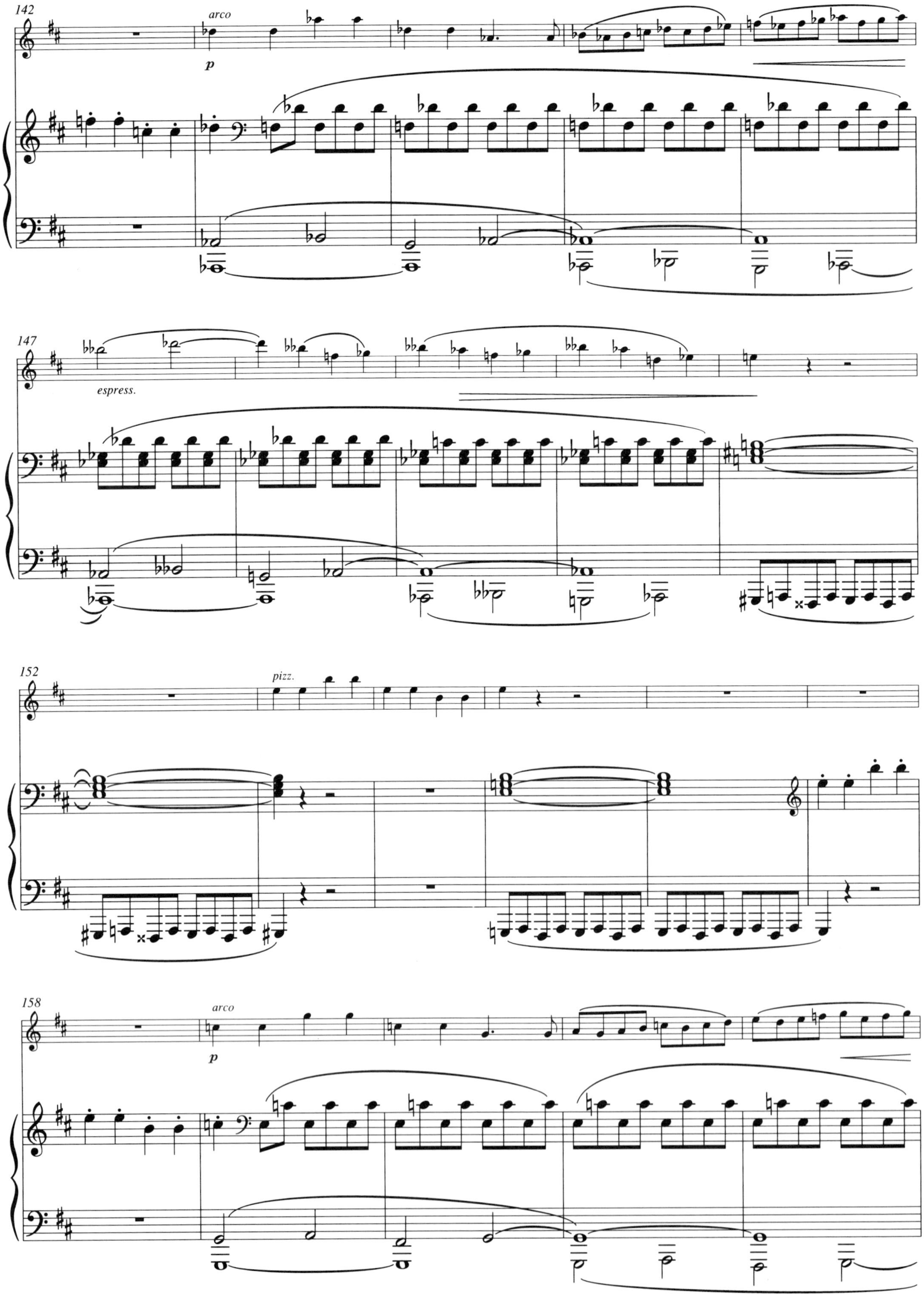
142
arco
p
147
espress.
152
pizz.
158
arco
p

155

156

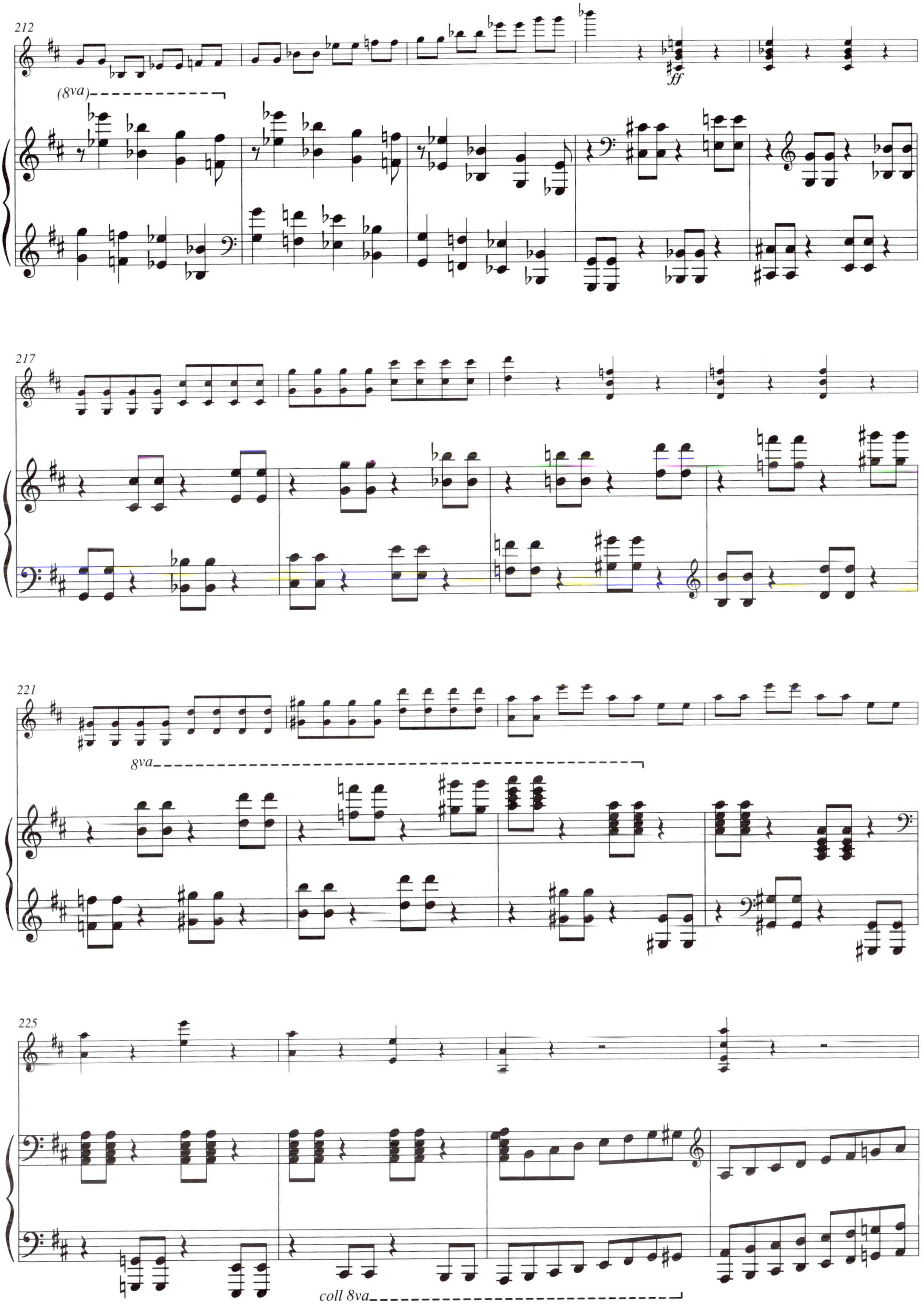
212
(8va)
ff
217
221
8va
225
coll 8va

158

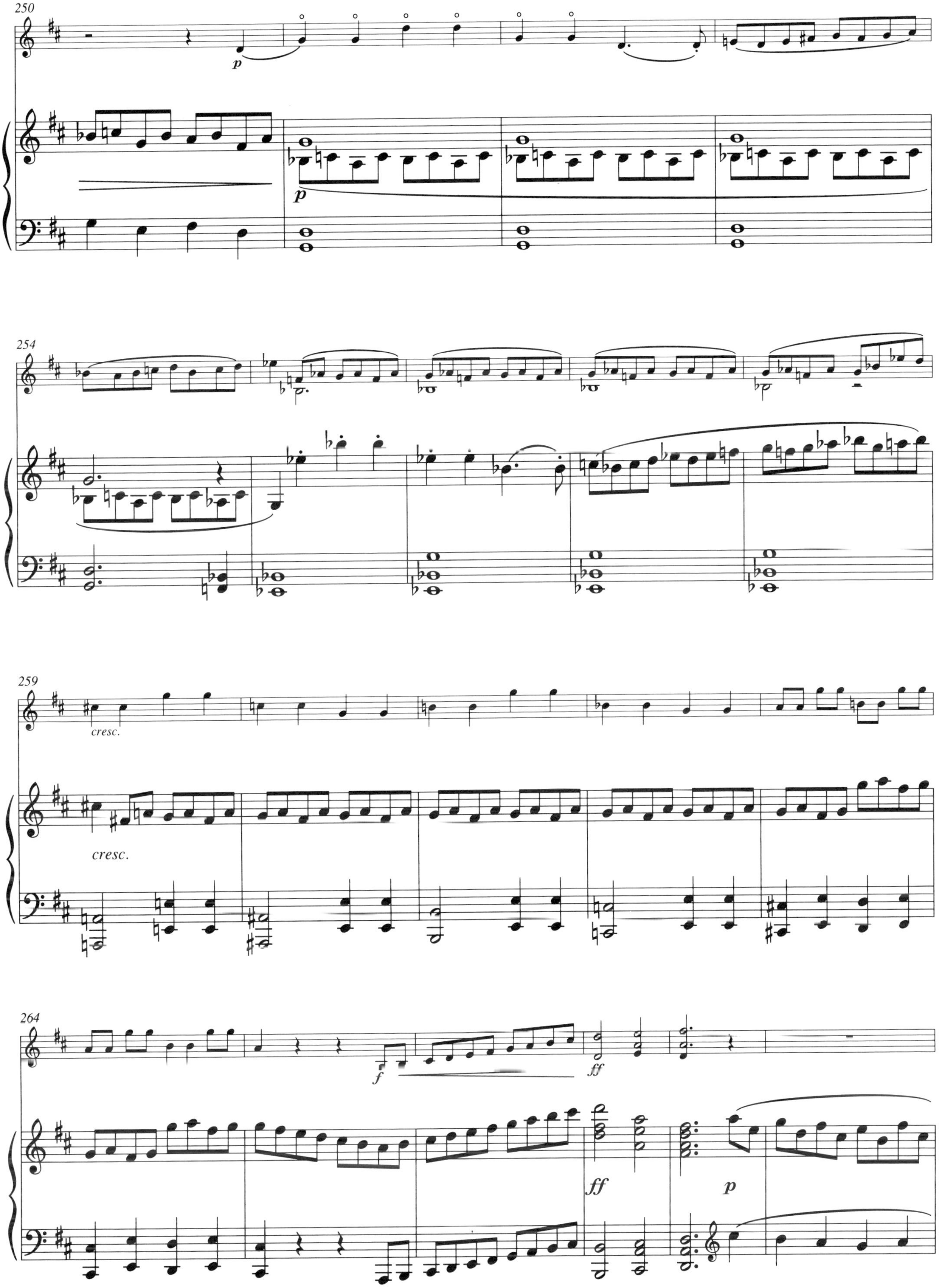
250
p
p
254
259
cresc.
cresc.
264
f
ff
ff
p

270
ff
ff
p
pizz.
p
276
arco
pizz.
280
arco
mf espress.
286
p
rit.
gliss.
a tempo
rit.
a tempo
p espress.

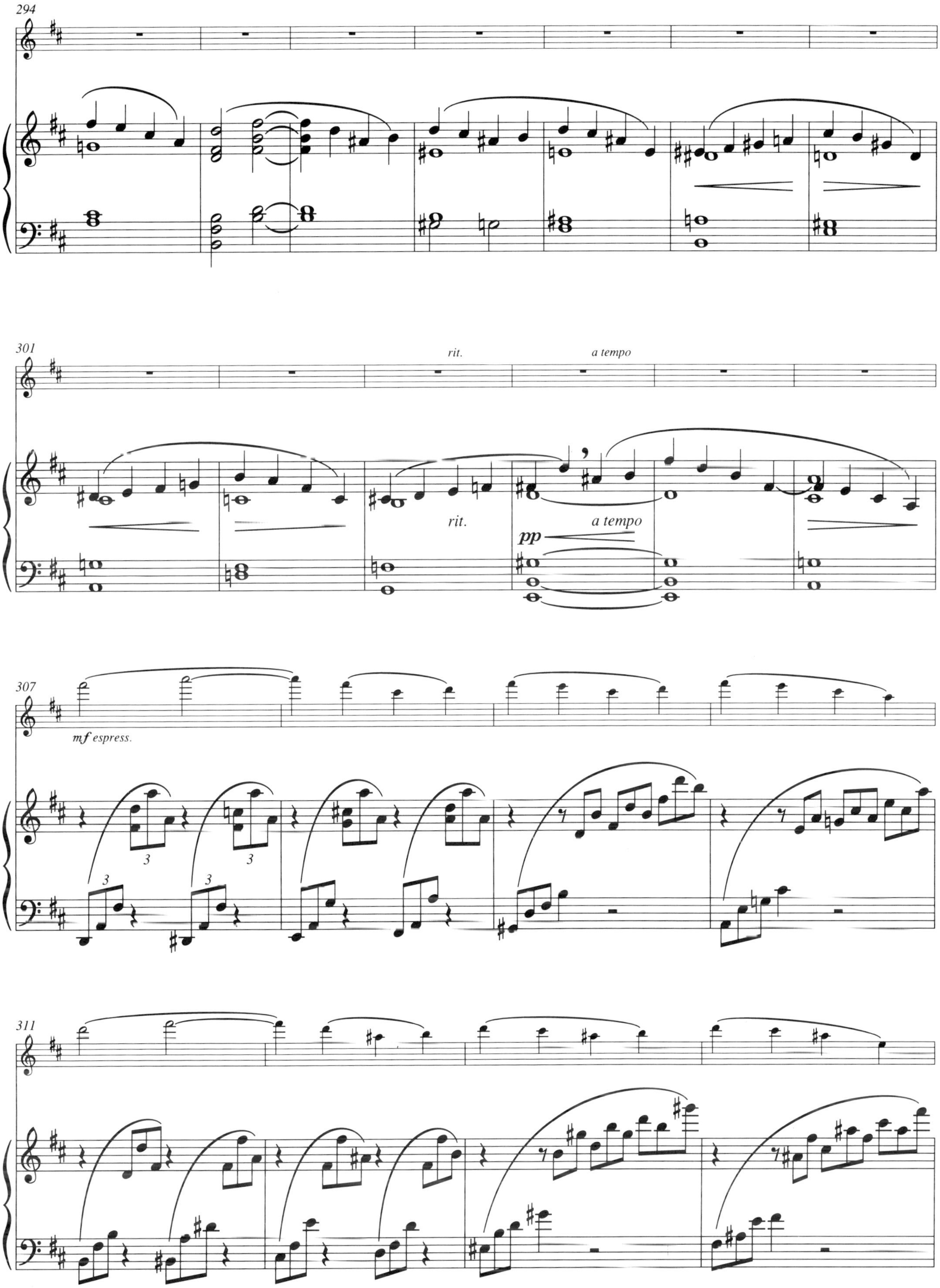
294
301
rit.
a tempo
rit.
pp
a tempo
307
mf espress.
3
3
3
3
311

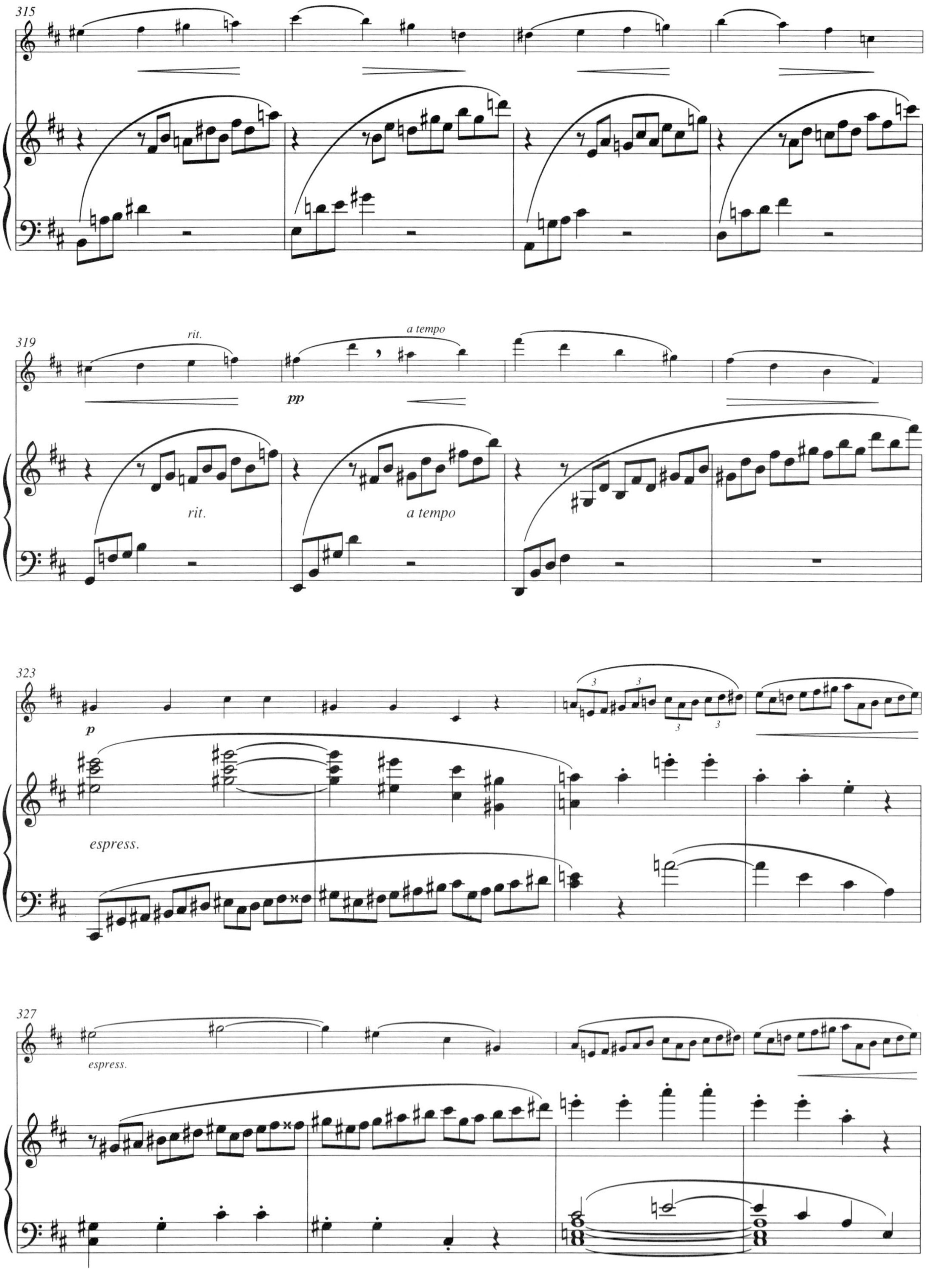
315
319
rit.
a tempo
pp
rit.
a tempo
323
p
espress.
327
espress.

163

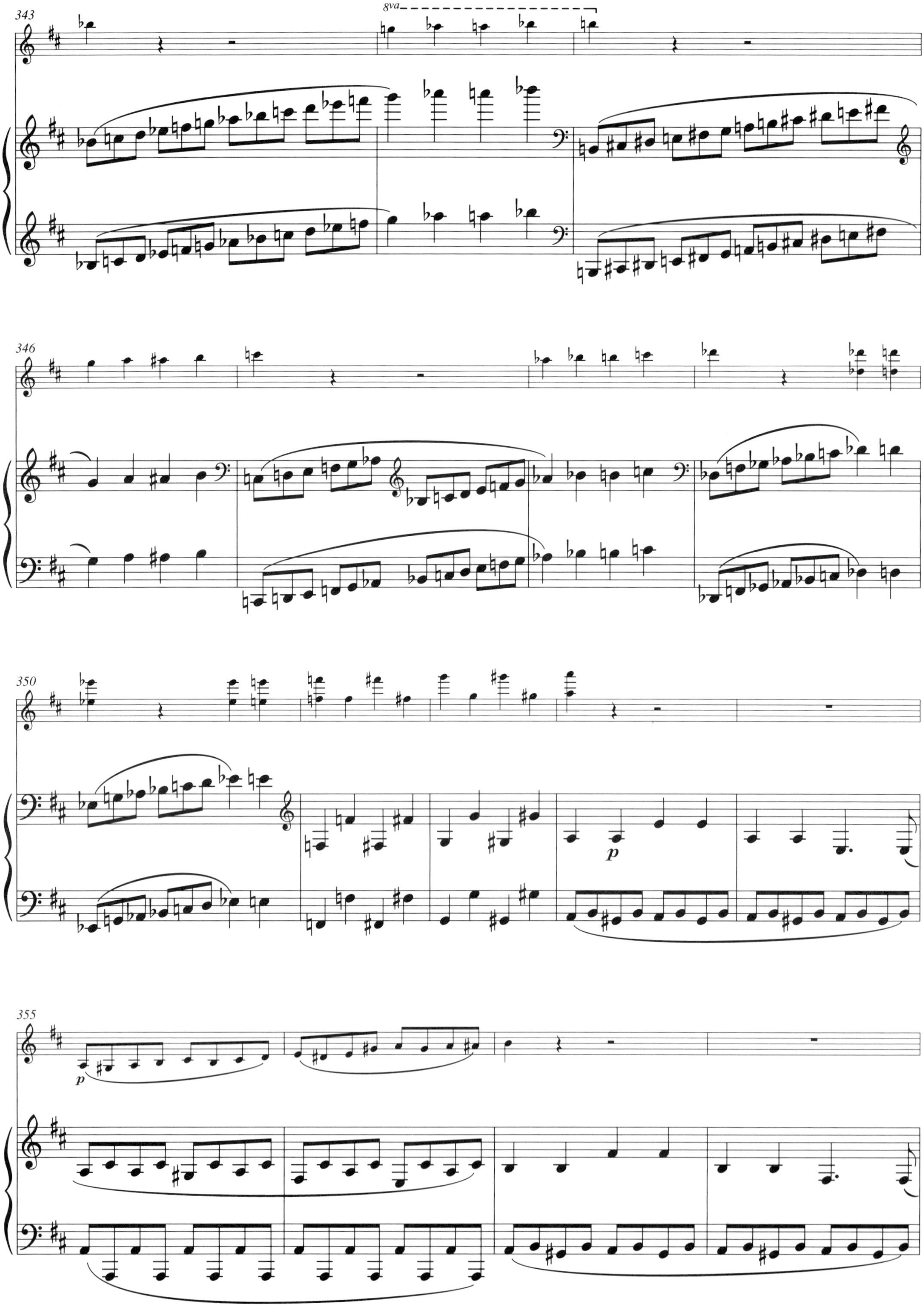
343
8va
346
350
p
355
p

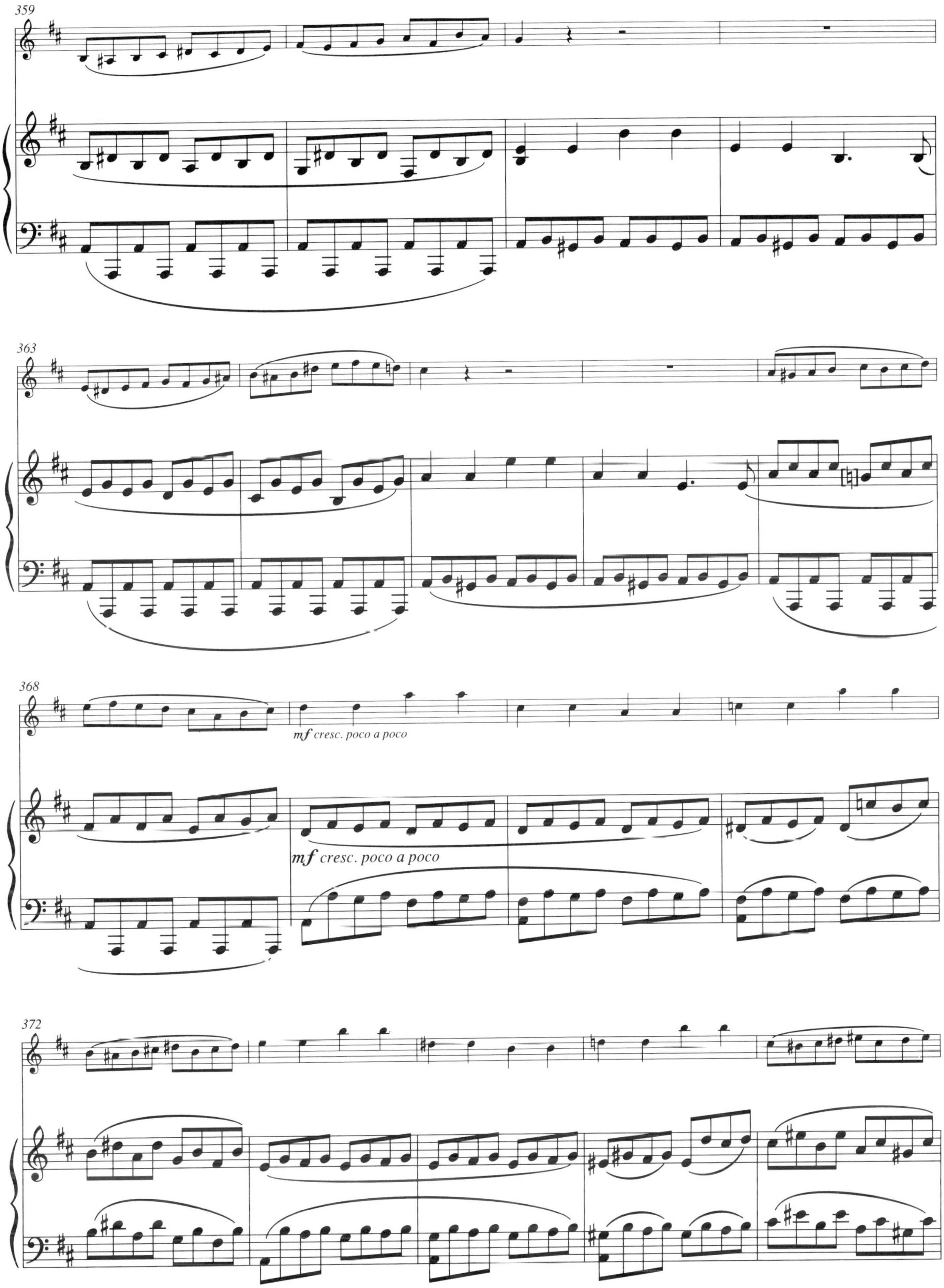
359
363
368
mf cresc. poco a poco
mf cresc. poco a poco
372

377
f
f
381
8va
Poco più mosso
(8va)
385
ff
ff
ff
string.
string.
8va
coll 8va
393
3

167

Appendix 1

Viola Part for the Quartet, Op. 1

I

Bratsche

Bratsche

Bratsche

Bratsche

IV

Allegro con brio

Bratsche

Bratsche

Below is a list of suggested editorial changes to the Quartet, op. 1 viola part. Metronome indications and other minor notational changes, such as the addition of a double bar to the end of a movement, have not been noted. Changes to cue parts are also not indicated.

I

M. 6, remove hairpin. M. 7, add decrescendo hairpin, from start of bar across the barline. M. 24, notes 2–3, add slur. M. 33, change *ff* to *f*. M. 41, remove quarter rest on beat 1; change half note to dotted half note. M. 50, note 1, add *ff*. M. 70, extend hairpin to begin on m. 69, note 1. Mm. 75–76, extend hairpin to end of m. 76. Mm. 79–80, remove "poco rit."; add "rit." at m. 80. Mm. 119–120, add "*f* con fuoco" beginning m. 119, note 1. Mm. 122–23, add crescendo hairpin from m. 122, note 1, to end of m. 123. Mm. 126–27, add crescendo hairpin from m. 126, note 1, to end of m. 127. M. 129, move *ff* from note 1 to note 2. M. 132, remove hairpin. M. 145, add "espress." after *mf*. Mm. 155–56, change *f* to *mf*; move hairpin to begin after *mf* and end at m. 156. M. 157, add *p*. M. 175, remove slur. M. 177, remove *p*. M. 182, change last note to e♭. Mm. 186–87, change *f* to *mf*; add crescendo hairpin from m. 186, after *mf*, to m. 187, note 3. M. 189, note 2, add *f*. M. 210, note 1, add *ff*. M. 218, change dotted half note to quarter rest, half note. Mm. 229–30, extend hairpin from m. 229, note 1, to m. 230, note 3. M. 277, remove "vivo." Mm. 287–92, remove hairpin. Mm. 293–94, change *ff* to *fff*; remove slur. M. 299, add decrescendo hairpin to entire bar. M. 309, change *mf* to *p*. M. 314, note 1, move *ff* to m. 313, note 1.

II

M. 9, remove "espr."; remove staccatos over notes 2–3. M. 11, notes 3–4, remove slur; notes 4–6, add slur. M. 14, notes 1–5, remove slur; notes 6–7, remove slur; replace with one slur over notes 1–7; M. 27, note 2, add "scherzando"; note 4, add staccato. M. 28, note 3, add staccato. M. 29, note 1, add *f*. M. 31, add crescendo hairpin to entire bar. M. 32, note 1, add *ff*. M. 38, remove hairpin. M. 39, remove *mf*. M. 47, change *f* to *mf*. M. 48, extend hairpin back to note 1. Mm. 48–49, remove slur from m. 48, note 3, to m. 49, note 1. M. 66, note 1, add "rit."; remove "poco rit." M. 73, note 1, add *f*. M. 76, note 1, change *p* to *pp*; note 4, add *p*; remove "poco a poco." Mm. 77–86, remove dotted line over staff. M. 78, remove *mf*. M. 79, add "più string."; remove "cresc."; add *mf* at note 2. M. 80, add "e cresc." M. 84, change *f* to "*ff* con fuoco." Mm. 85–86, remove hairpin. M. 88, change lowest note on final chord to quarter note. M. 90, change lowest note on final chord to quarter note. M. 91, extend slur on notes 2–4 to begin on note 1; add slur over notes 5–7. M. 95, remove "dim."; add "espress." after *p*. M. 96, notes 2–3, add decrescendo hairpin. M. 97, note 2, add crescendo hairpin. M. 98, note 1, add decrescendo hairpin; notes 2–3, add crescendo hairpin. M. 99, notes 1–2, add decrescendo hairpin. M. 101, move *pp* to m. 100, note 3.

III

M. 6, note 2, change to eighth note followed by eighth-note rest. M. 8, move "rit." to m. 9, note 1. M. 9, extend slur back to m. 8, note 3. M. 11, move "a tempo" to m. 10, eighth rest; add *p* at chord. M. 15, beat 1, add "cresc." M. 17, add *pp* at chord. M. 19, change *f* to *mf*; add crescendo hairpin to entire bar. Mm. 21–22, add crescendo hairpin from m. 21, note 4, to m. 22, note 3. M. 23, change *f* to *mf*; add crescendo hairpin from note 1 to end of bar. M. 24, note 1, add *f*. Mm. 26–27, remove slur across barline. M. 29, add crescendo hairpin from *p* to end of bar. M. 30, notes 1–2, add decrescendo hairpin. M. 31, note 1, add *p*. M. 34, add *pp* at chord. M. 35, add "Tempo I." M. 39, notes 1–2, add crescendo hairpin. M. 40, note 1–2, add crescendo hairpin. M. 41, move "rit." to beginning of measure; note 1, add *pp*. M. 43, move "a tempo" to m. 42, last eighth-note rest. M. 46, change *f* to *mf*. M. 58, change *pp* to *p*. Mm. 60–61, add slur from m. 60, note 1, to m. 61, note 3.

IV

M. 2, change note 8 to eighth note followed by eighth-note rest. M. 6, add *p* to note 1. M. 10, notes 5–6, remove slashes through stems. M. 15, add *f* to note 1. M. 19, move hairpin to extend from m. 19, note 7, to m. 20, note 3. M. 22, move "cresc." to note 1. Mm. 23–24, begin hairpin at m. 24. M. 24, note 1, add *f*; change two-note slurs to four-note slurs. M. 25, move *ff* from note 1 to note 2. M. 26, add natural to e. M. 37, notes 1–3, add crescendo hairpin. M. 38, add decrescendo hairpin to entire bar. M. 40, add *p* before hairpin. M. 43, remove *mf*. M. 44, extend hairpin to begin on note 1. M. 46, remove *p*. M. 47, note 1, add *mf*. M. 55, note 2, add *f*. M. 59, note 1, move *ff* to m. 58, note 2. M. 63, note 1, add *ff*. M. 68, extend hairpin to begin at m. 67, note 2 and end at m. 68, note 2. M. 69, add *pp*. M. 70, remove *pp*. M. 79, note 1, add *p*. Mm. 79–82, add slurs to sixteenth-note pairs throughout. M. 82, add crescendo hairpin to begin at m. 82, note 1 and end at m. 83, note 1. M. 94, add *p* to note 5. M. 97, add crescendo hairpin to entire bar. Mm. 99–100, remove hairpin. M. 101, remove *ff*. M. 113, note 1, add *mf*. M. 115, notes 1–7, remove slur; notes 1–3, add slur; notes 4–7, add slur; note 4, add *f*. M. 117, note 1, add *p*; notes 1–7, remove slur; notes 1–3, add slur; notes 4–7, add slur; end hairpin before note 4; notes 4–7, add decrescendo hairpin. M. 118, remove hairpin. M. 119, add crescendo hairpin from *pp* to end of bar. M. 120, add decrescendo hairpin to entire bar. M. 121, beats 3–4, add crescendo hairpin. M. 122, add decrescendo hairpin to entire bar. M. 127, move *ff* to m. 126, note 1. M. 130, remove "scherzando." M. 138, change *f* to *mf*. M. 139, note 1, change to dotted quarter note. M. 142, change from two-note to four-note slurs. Mm. 144–45, remove tie across barline. M. 152, remove *p*. Mm. 158–59, add three-note slur to each triplet grouping. M. 159, add crescendo hairpin to entire bar. M. 160, add decrescendo hairpin to entire bar. M. 161, remove "cresc."; add crescendo hairpin to entire bar. M. 162, add decrescendo hairpin to entire bar. M. 163, add decrescendo hairpin after *mf* to end of bar. M. 164, notes 1–4, add decrescendo hairpin. M. 170, change *mf* to *p*. Mm. 172–73, add crescendo hairpin from m. 172, note 5, to end of m. 173. M. 174, notes 1–4, add decrescendo hairpin. M. 176, change *f* to *mf*. Mm. 177–78, add crescendo hairpin from m. 177, note 1, to m. 178, last note. Mm. 183–86, change *mf* to *ff*; remove hairpin. M. 187, remove *f*. M. 191, add "al fine" after *ff*. M. 197, remove *ff*. M. 199, remove "*ff* al fine."

Appendix 2

Catalog of Walter Rabl's Published Works

Op. 1

Quartett für Pianoforte, Clarinette (oder Bratsche), Violine und Violoncell (Berlin: Simrock, 1897) [Dasselbe, für Pianoforte zu Vier Händen]

Op. 2

Fantasiestücke für Clavier, Violine und Violoncell (Berlin: Simrock, 1897) [Zwei Hefte]

Op. 3

Vier Lieder für eine Singstimme mit Begleitung des Pianoforte. Für hohe und für tiefe Stimme (Berlin: Simrock, 1897) [1. *Schön Rothraut*, 2. *Lied vom Winde*, 3. *Triftiger Grund*, 4. *Die Tochter der Haide*]

Op. 4

Vier Lieder für eine Singstimme mit Begleitung des Pianoforte. Für hohe und für tiefe Stimme (Berlin: Simrock, 1897) [1. *Mädchenlied* "O Blätter, dürre Blätter," 2. "Es geht ein lindes Wehen," 3. *Am fliessenden Wasser* "Hell im Silberlichte," 4. "Und hast du die Lippen"]

Op. 5

Vier Lieder für eine Singstimme mit Klavier und Violoncell (Berlin: Simrock, 1899) [English translation by Constance Bache] [1. *Zu spät*, 2. *Vorbei*, 3. *Spielmannslied*, 4. *Soldatentod*]

Op. 6

Sonate für Pianoforte und Violine (Berlin: Simrock, 1899)

Op. 7

Drei Lieder für eine Singstimme mit Begleitung des Pianoforte (Berlin: Simrock, 1899) [English translation by Constance Bache] [1. *Jägers Liebe*, 2. *Der stille Trinker*, 3. *Schifferliedchen*]

Op. 8

Symphonie (D moll) für grosses Orchester (Berlin: Simrock, 1899) [Dasselbe, für Pianoforte zu Vier Händen]

Op. 9

Frau Sehnsucht. Dichtung von Wilhelm Eberhard Ernst. Für 1 Singstimme mit Pianoforte. Komplett (Leipzig: D. Rahter, n.d.) [1. *Nachtklänge* "Meine Sehnsucht schwang sich," 2. *Des Wassers Stimmen* "Es drängt sich brausend," 3. *Frühsonnenlicht* "Das ist ein Wispern und Raunen," 4. *Regenwanderung* "Tropfen rieseln von den Zweigen," 5. *Stilles Gewähren* "Nein, sage mir nicht," 6. *Märchen* "Nun ward es still," 7. *Dunkelnde Pfade* "Oft gehst du in Träumen," 8. *Des Märchens Ende* "Das Lied ist verklungen," 9. *Zu spät!* "Ich hab' dich bezaubert"]

Op. 10

6 Gedichte von Anna Ritter, für 1 Singstimme mit Pianoforte. Für hohe und für tiefe Stimme: Komplett (Leipzig: D. Rahter, n.d.) [1. *Im Waldesfrieden* "Tiefer, tiefer Waldesfrieden," 2. "Ich hab' an seiner Brust geruht," 3. "Wie ein Rausch ist deine Liebe," 4. *Schlafe, ach schlafe* "Und dürft' ich dich wecken," 5. *Weißt du's noch?* "Unter den blühenden Linden," 6. *Sehnsucht nach dem Geliebten* "Um dich hab' ich die ganze Nacht"]

Op. 11

"Wo der Weg zum Liebchen geht." *Gedicht von Rudolf Baumbach. Für Tenor mit Orchester- oder Pianofortebegleitung. Für hohe und für tiefe Stimme. Orchester-Partitur und Stimmen in Abschrift* (Leipzig: D. Rahter, n.d.)

Op. 12

Neue Liebe: "Hinaus ins Weite," von Emanuel Geibel. Für vierstimmigen Männerchor und Tenorsolo mit Begleitung des Pianoforte und 4 Hörnern ad lib. Partitur und chorstimmen (Leipzig: D. Rahter, 1902)

Op. 13

Sturmlieder. Gedichte von Anna Ritter. Für Sopran mit Orchester- oder Pianofortebegleitung. Orchesterpartitur in Abschrift. Orchesterstimmen in Abschrift. Ausgabe mit Pianoforte. Für hohe und für tiefe Stimme: Komplett (Leipzig: D. Rahter, n.d.) [1. *Sturmflut* "Die Wogenrosse schäumen," 2. *Sturmeswerben* "Hei! wie er tobt," 3. *Märzensturm* "Märzensturm, rufst du mich?," 4. "Ich wollt', ich wär des Sturmes Weib"]

Op. 14

Never published

Op. 15

Zwei Lieder für eine Singstimme mit Klavier (Leipzig: D. Rahter, n.d.) [1. *Ich liebe dich* "Ich reiße dich aus meinem Herzen" von Anna Ritter, 2. *Passion* "Mein Lieb, ich träumte seltsam heut" von Paul Althof]

No Opus Number

Liane. Dichtung in einem Vorspiel und drei Aufzügen (Strasbourg: Süddeutscher Musikverlag, 1903)